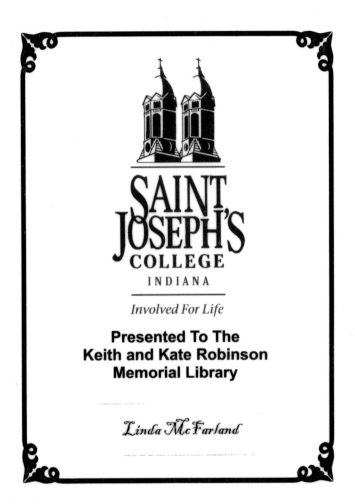

SAINT JOSEPH'S
COLLEGE
INDIANA

Involved For Life

**Presented To The
Keith and Kate Robinson
Memorial Library**

Linda McFarland

THE ETHICAL EDGE

TALES OF ORGANIZATIONS THAT HAVE FACED MORAL CRISES

DAWN-MARIE DRISCOLL, W. MICHAEL HOFFMAN

EDWARD PETRY

HERITAGE

IMPRINT

MasterMedia Limited
New York, N.Y.

MASTERMEDIA and colophon are registered trademarks of
MasterMedia Limited.

p.   cm.

ISBN 1-57101-053-3 : $24.95

95-000000

CIP

Designed by Virginia Koenke Hunt

Manufactured in the United States of America

For

Norman and Christopher

Josephine and Bliss

and

Joan, Joe, Steve, and Tom

Acknowledgments

The Ethical Edge would not have been possible without the help of many. We would like to thank those who shared insights and experiences to ensure that the tales in this book would convey the whole story and be both accurate and fair.

In particular we would like to thank the ethics officers and managers from organizations featured in the text. Without their commitment to business ethics, there would be no tales to tell. We thank and we applaud the ongoing work of: Harry Britt and Kevin Gildart of Bath Iron Works; Graydon Wood, Jacquelyn Gates, Ann Whelehen, and Richard Warren of NYNEX; Keith Darcy and Jim Settel of Prudential Securities; Fred Verinder and Andy Koczon of LABCORP; Shirley Peterson and Frank Daly of Northrop Grumman; Michael Jackson of Dow Corning; and Cheryle Wills from United Way. We would like also to thank Joe McHugh of Bentley College, whose case study formed a basis for our telling of the Bath Iron Works tale, and John Swanson, formerly of Dow Corning, who provided important context and insights for the still unfolding breast implant controversy.

The staff of the Solomon Baker Library at Bentley College,

Kate Sullivan of Bentley College, and Carol Roark of the Dallas Public Library all provided valuable research assistance during the earlier stages of this project.

For their administrative support throughout the writing of this book, we would like to thank Mary Chiasson, Kelly LeBlanc, Jill Callinan, Vickie Iwasa, and Kim Smith. Oscar and Grace St. Thomas occasionally provided a quiet place to write and think away from phones and fax machines. And, finally, our thanks to Bentley College, the Center for Business Ethics, and the Ethics Officer Association for allowing us the flexibility to complete this project.

DAWN-MARIE DRISCOLL
W. MICHAEL HOFFMAN
EDWARD PETRY

TABLE OF CONTENTS

Introduction

DISCOVERING THE ETHICAL EDGE

- What can managers and employees do when faced with an ethical dilemma on the job?
- What are the latest ethics "best practices" in nonprofit and profit organizations? What are companies such as NYNEX, Texas Instruments, Northrop Grumman, and others doing to help build an ethical culture into their daily operations?
- What lessons can be learned from organizations that have faced moral crises and recovered successfully?
- What are some of the ethical problems, trends and regulatory changes to watch out for in upcoming years?

In this book we've collected tales of organizations that have faced moral crises: serious violations of their standards of conduct, improprieties by their executives, and illegalities by their employees. These scandals resulted in front page publicity, firings, jail terms, and plummeting corporate values. But the news is not all bad. We've chosen stories that highlight all of the tough lessons organizations have learned, and the "best practices" they've put in place to prevent future problems. We've also included a few stories about organizations that may not have learned their lessons in spite of the problems they've already encountered.

In addition to our tales, we offer tips, advice, and checklists designed especially for managers who are responsible for actually developing an ethical culture for their organization. Our stories also present examples of "best practices" from organizations that are leaders in the field of business ethics.

Our hope in collecting these tales is that we will help organizations discover **the ethical edge** that can ensure them a solid future, that can keep them from getting too close to the brink and falling into a moral crisis. We believe there are concrete, practical steps that any organization can and should take to help prevent costly ethical problems. For those problems that are not entirely preventable, we want to facilitate a speedy recovery for the organization and to offer strategies for becoming better prepared to handle the next crisis lurking down the road. These practical steps will enable organizations to gain **the ethical edge,** and at the same time become more competitive and financially successful in the long run.

We decided to write this book because we've seen too many savvy and otherwise knowledgeable business leaders who knew their organizations were in a moral crisis but were unaware that other organizations had faced and had successfully recovered from similar problems. In many cases these leaders knew something about business ethics but dismissed the whole subject as too idealistic, or impractical, or only for do-gooders. While help was at hand, their lack of information, or their cynicism, or both, prevented them from reaching for it.

This book is not just for senior managers, though. We've also seen employees at all levels who have encountered ethical dilemmas and had no one to turn to for guidance: a laborer for a construction subcontractor who observes his supervisors paying bribes to inspectors to get the job inspected this week rather than next month; a secretary who makes purchases at a large office supply store for her nonprofit employer and who keeps for herself the additional discount coupons given at the cash register; an advertising account manager who is told by a printer, "Sure we'll redo your job at no cost to correct your error, but all future printing business for your clients belongs to us."

In some cases, the rudderless employee is a client or sales representative or an independent contractor or entrepreneur. In a world where commerce is becoming more complex every day, even the solo operator is seeking **the ethical edge.**

The business environment is changing rapidly. The 90s are not the 80s, and the next decade will be just as different. Public expectations are higher; common practices from a few years ago are now considered unethical; regulatory agencies are more demanding; industry standards are rising; new employees are more cynical; sentencing guidelines have increased potential fines; senior executives now face jail terms; international customs vary; and the list goes on. In short, the number of potential ethical problems has increased and the risks have never been greater. Many examples of good companies that have suddenly found themselves in serious trouble could be cited, but one will do for now—a story that proves that ethical lapses cut a wide swath of victims.

Consider the case of Prudential Securities, whose agents sold risky limited partnerships to 340,000 investors. Many of the investors did not understand the product, which is generally suitable only for wealthy individuals. The "costliest scandal in Wall Street history" nearly destroyed the company's reputation while costing Prudential Securities almost $2 billion in legal expenses and compensation to victims. The careers of several executives ended and the company was put on probation for three years. Prudential Securities appointed a new corporate ethics officer and, through training and other initiatives, is trying to reform its corporate culture. Its story is included in this book.

The tales we have chosen are important not just for their drama, pathos, and intrigue—although they certainly contain those. More to the point, our stories raise issues and questions with which business people in all industries, all across the country are struggling:

- **What can an organization do to protect itself from serious indiscretions by senior management?**

We'll look at how the United Way of America reacted to rumors that its highly respected CEO was using company assets to carry on a globetrotting affair with a teenager. We'll compare the United Way to some other nonprofits and for-profit organizations, including Bath Iron Works of Maine. BIW reevaluated the role of its board of directors and established ethics committees and an ethics office to help oversee the conduct of senior management. We'll examine corporate strategies for building an internal reporting system—commonly called a hotline, or helpline—and the problems that such a system can create, including whether or not such a system is useful in cases where senior management is the problem.

- **What steps can an organization take to ensure that its employees do not feel overly pressured to set aside ethics and the long-term interests of the company?**

Prudential Securities is certainly one example of this type of problem; in fact, the investment world in general has yet to face the problem created by its compensation and bonus systems that reward sales volume over client service. Similar problems are commonplace. We'll examine models for ethics initiatives at several companies, all of which have had to deal with ethical problems that resulted from the fact that employees believed they were being pressured to act contrary to their own consciences and against corporate ethics policies.

- **What can an organization do to help ensure that its values and traditions are understood and embraced by a new generation of employees and by employees overseas?**

General Electric and Texas Instruments have developed innovative ethics training and communication strategies. We'll look at what companies are doing to help keep the ethics message fresh and firmly establish the idea that adherence to ethics remains a priority even in tough times.

- **How does an organization maintain a balance between enforcing rules and maintaining compliance while at the same time encouraging entrepreneurship and autonomy?**

Perhaps surprisingly, not all ethics programs get high marks. We'll discuss the problems created by organizations that—in an effort to meet rising regulatory standards or in reaction to problems in their past—have become gun-shy, have built unnecessary ethics and compliance bureaucracies, and have unintentionally created additional ethical problems.

Taken together, the lessons in this book can be thought of as a blueprint for **organizational moral excellence.** Many organizations today have already written a code of ethics. Unfortunately, too often, that is the extent of their ethics effort. A code is an important first step, but it is just that—a first step. To be effective, to ensure its adequate communication, oversight, enforcement, adjudication, and review, it must be backed up by support structures throughout the entire organization. And for this a blueprint is needed; a plan for building an ethical culture.

While it is true that you can't build a sound structure without a well-designed blueprint, it's also true that blueprints usually have to be changed to accommodate the specific problems that arise during the on-site construction. Learning how to adapt the blueprint to the real-world situation is a skill that must be acquired by a good architectural engineer through experience. So too in this case.

Ideas for an organizational ethical blueprint can be suggested by others or learned by studying the experiences of others; ultimately, however, this is a project that can only be done by the organization itself. We hope our stories will inspire, motivate and encourage readers to discover **the ethical edge.** We also hope this will lead to a process of self-construction involving redevelopment and remodeling. But, of course, in advance of the structural design and the start of construction, the organization must first decide that it needs and is willing to make the investment in the ethical building.

Before we turn to our tales, we will set the stage by addressing three of the common myths that many still believe about business ethics. Once we have dispensed with these myths, we can then turn to the practical issues of developing an enduring and effective organizational ethics initiative to achieve **the ethical edge.**

SECTION ONE

FIRST THINGS FIRST

1 Debunking the Myths

2 Quiz Yourself
on Business Ethics

3 How Do You Make
Ethical Business Decisions?

DEBUNKING THE MYTHS

Perhaps you've heard, or even voiced yourself, these persistent myths about business ethics:

● Business ethics is an oxymoron, a contradiction in terms.

● Business ethics is a fad, the latest managerial "flavor of the month."

● Ethics is entirely a personal matter. Employees are either ethical individuals or they are not. An organization can't have ethics.

Myth #1

Business ethics is an oxymoron, a contradiction in terms.

In the mid-1980s, a *Wall Street Journal* front-page story called business ethics "an oxymoron, a contradiction in terms like jumbo shrimp." One can certainly understand why the *Wall Street Journal* would be so cynical; because the headlines of the 80s, without question, appeared to support such a conclusion. The popular press often had a difficult time deciding which scandal to feature. The decade of the 80s began with international bribery scandals, and these were quickly followed by reports of $600 hammers and "waste, fraud, and abuse" in the defense industry. Before the dust could settle on these cases, we were buried in stories of hostile takeovers made possible by fee-hungry Wall Street firms but felt most sharply on Main Street. Banking deregulation opened up neighborhood S&Ls to land speculators and con artists.

By the middle of the decade, insider trading, greenmail and poison pills were common themes in popular movies, and the inside stories of Dennis Levine and other white collar criminals were best-sellers. In simpler times, the men and women who captured the nation's attention were its movie stars, astronauts, politicians, and sports heroes. In the 1980s, though, the nation became fascinated by its wheelers and dealers. We were drawn to the stories of T. Boone Pickens, F. Ross Johnson, Sir James Goldsmith and other high-rollers who seemed to stay on the right side of the law while taking apart long-established companies. And, perhaps even more so, we were fascinated by the stories of those who clearly crossed the ethical and legal line — including Ivan Boesky, Charles Keating, and Michael Milken.

Given all this, it is perhaps not surprising that so many people in the 1980s believed "business ethics" truly was an oxymoron and that for business executives the bottom line was the only measure of values. We hear the oxymoron joke much less these days. Thoughtful individuals have come to understand that when talking about business ethics, no one is claiming that business is always ethical. Our claim is that business can and should be scrutinized from an ethical point of view. That is the whole idea behind business ethics.

Some skeptics, however, persist. They argue: "What we mean

in saying that business ethics is an oxymoron is that business and ethics shouldn't mix. Business is business. Ethical considerations are not appropriate in business." This is an even more troubling position. Is it true? Is business somehow immune from ethics? When we're at work, are we somehow exempt from the ethical standards that apply during the rest of our lives?

Many people seem to think so. Business professor Theodore Levitt once wrote in the prestigious *Harvard Business Review*: "Business must fight as if it were at war. And, like a good war, it should be fought gallantly, daringly, and above all not morally." Those who argue in favor of this point of view usually qualify it by acknowledging that business must abide by the "rules of the game," which includes laws and regulations; but they also insist that businesses do not have a duty to go beyond what is required by law.

This attitude is dramatically illustrated by a famous case in business ethics: the Ford Pinto. In 1978, three young women were burned to death when the Pinto they were driving was struck from the rear and the gas tank exploded. The Ford Motor Company was subsequently indicted and tried on charges of criminal homicide — a first in the annals of corporate history. In his instructions to the jury, the judge said that Ford should be convicted if it could be shown that it had engaged in "plain, conscious and unjustifiable disregard of harm that might result (from its actions) and the disregard involves a substantial deviation from acceptable standards of conduct." In 1980, the jury returned a verdict of not guilty.

Though the Ford Motor Company was cleared of criminal charges in a court of law, it lost in the court of public opinion and subsequently paid out millions of dollars in civil suits. Ford knew that the Pinto gas tank was vulnerable to rear-end collisions, and it had figured out how to remedy the defect. In fact, Ford had conducted a cost-benefit analysis comparing the benefits to society of Ford paying for burn deaths and injuries versus the costs of making the Pinto gas tank safer. The study concluded that it would be less costly for the company to pay for the deaths and injuries even though the safety changes needed would cost only $11 per car. Despite this knowledge, attorneys for Ford tried to show that Ford neither unjustifiably disregarded harm nor deviated from acceptable standards of conduct. One of their main arguments was that the Pinto met all applicable safety laws and regulations and was comparable to other cars of the same type. They argued that the Pinto was in compliance with the law, and therefore nothing further could be required of the company.

Today students of the Pinto case understand that business ethics is not the same as compliance with the law. The law provides the floor, or the lowest agreed upon standard below which one should not go. While laws are intended to be ethical and to be based on some consensus of what is right, ethics is a much broader category. Ethics is the study of what is good and right for people. Ethics is about not causing unjustifiable harm. It is about doing only what you would be willing to have done to you. Ethics asks the question: How should I act toward others, especially when their interests are at stake? It has been said that being ethical requires doing more than you're required to do, and less than you're allowed to do.

Many examples could be given of products and services that meet legal requirements yet are known by the companies that produce them to be potentially hazardous. In some cases, such as the Pinto one, the manufacturer also knows how to eliminate or minimize the hazards. The fact that companies possess this type of information but often choose not to act on it is good evidence that they believe they have no obligation to go beyond the law in preventing harm.

One reason why business people may feel no ethical obligation to go beyond the law was summed up by Milton Friedman, the Nobel Prize-winning economist. In 1970 he wrote: "There is one and only one social responsibility of business — to use its resources and engage in activities designed to increase its profits...." But there is more to Friedman's argument than meets the eye. He explained his belief that ethics should not have a high priority in business in the following way:

"In a free-enterprise, private-property system, a corporate executive is an employee of the owners of the business. He has direct responsibility to his employers. That responsibility is to conduct the business in accordance with their desires," says the economist, "which generally will be to make as much money as possible while conforming to the basic rules of society, both those embodied in law and those embodied in ethical custom."

Friedman's argument has usually been misinterpreted as a rejection of ethics in business. It obviously is not. He acknowledges that business should conform to legal and ethical "rules of society." Unfortunately, he doesn't go beyond a kind of "ethical minimalism," which gives a low priority to ethics and a much higher priority to "profit maximization." He believes this is what owners (the stockholders) demand, and that managers have a moral duty to carry out the wishes of owners, who, in his opinion, choose maximizing profits over ethics. His notion is that shareholders, not stakeholders, are the primary concern of business institutions.

Is he right? We don't think so. The issue is not that simple. While it is of course necessary for business to be profitable, we believe there is also a growing consensus that business should be held ethically accountable. The bar has been raised. The public, including shareholders, now demand more; they demand that profits be obtained in an ethical manner.

Since the 1970s, public opinion has shifted tremendously on this issue. There was a general acceptance of business practices in the 50s and 60s. During that time, few ethical questions were raised and a concern for profit maximization did seem to be the be-all and end-all. Then, following the Pinto and similar cases, widespread cynicism about business set in. Today the emerging view can perhaps best be characterized as a mix combining heightened scrutiny of businesses' ethical practices with a cautious optimism that things can change. The current bottom line reality is that a moral or ethical crisis can affect a company's share price or an organization's reputation as much as a poor profit and loss sheet can.

Business leaders have been given an opportunity to improve the ethics of business voluntarily. For the time being no one is clamoring for further governmental action in this area — but that could change. The public is saying loud and clear: "We expect higher ethical standards, we won't tolerate ethical and legal wrongdoing, we want *you* (not government) to clean things up, and we expect you to take care of this and still remain profitable."

Prudent business executives have recognized this important shift in public opinion. They know that to remain competitive as well as to avoid future regulatory requirements, they must strive to meet the new, higher standard. Given the changes, ignoring ethics, or giving ethics a low priority, is to "run for luck."

This of course does not mean profit isn't a priority. What it does mean is that the public now demands a balance. The Business Roundtable recognized the importance of accounting for both profit and ethics. Its 1988 report "Corporate Ethics: A Prime Business Asset" says: "The corporate community should continue to refine and renew efforts to improve performance and manage change effectively through programs in corporate ethics.... Many corporate executives believe that a culture in which ethical concern permeates the whole organization is necessary to the self-interest of the company.... Corporate ethics is a strategic key to survival and profitability in this era of fierce competitiveness in a global economy."

And so it appears that Friedman was right, up to a point. Managers do have a duty to "conduct business in accordance with the desires of the owners." But he was not right in assuming that the owners didn't understand the impact of ethical conduct on the fiscal health of the institution.

Its important to remember that a concern for ethics must be weighed against other legitimate concerns. George Cabot Lodge once told a story of a businessman whose misdirected actions in the name of ethics actually did more harm than good.

At the Center for Business Ethics' First National Conference on Business Ethics in 1977, Lodge described a friend who owned a paper company on the banks of a New England stream. On the first Earth Day in 1970, his friend was converted to the cause of environmentalism. He became determined to stop his company's pollution of the stream, and marched off to put his newfound convictions into action.

Later, after learning that his friend had gone broke, Lodge visited him. Radiating a kind of "ethical" purity, the friend told Lodge that he had spent millions to stop the pollution but then could no longer compete with other paper companies that did not follow his shining example. His company went under. Five hundred people lost their jobs, and the stream remained polluted.

The friend's zealotry solved nothing. In fact, it did far more harm than good. The friend's approach was out of balance. He had lost perspective. He forgot that business ethics is ethics in a business context. In this case he might have been better off asking, "How can I have an impact on changing the unethical practices of my industry? Who can I build alliances with to get this moving?"

To gain the ethical edge we must not only meet ethical standards but we also need to keep in mind the practical demands of business. We know this can be done. In fact, as our stories in this book will show, there is ample evidence that it is al done in many organizations.

Myth #2

**Business ethics is a fad,
the latest managerial "flavor of the m**

Individuals have been concerned about tryin ethics of business for as long as there has been bus over business ethics is not new. Nearly four thousand the Code of Hammurabi records that Mesopotamian rulers attempted to establish honest prices. Some might say that the code was a bit harsh, though, in that it called for death for most infractions. The critique of the ethics of business continued. Aristotle, in the fourth century BC, discussed the virtues and vices of merchants and tradesmen, and the Old and New Testaments and the Koran often refer to ethics as it relates to wealth and poverty.

In the modern era, capitalism and its relationship to freedom and the "greater good" was an important theme in the writings of the utilitarian philosopher J.S. Mill. Even Adam Smith, who is known as an economist but was in fact the chair of moral philosophy at the University of Glasgow, wrote extensively on morality and capitalism. Thomas Jefferson, Ralph Waldo Emerson, and Henry David Thoreau were among numerous American statesmen and philosophers who compared and contrasted the values they associated with manufacturing against those of agriculture.

The 19th century saw a great increase in the attention being given to the ethics of business practices. Human rights issues, chief of which were slavery and child labor, were also the foremost business ethics issues of the century. Political and labor movements at the time continued their historical, ethical critique of capitalism. Throughout the century there was a gradual evolution of what was considered to be acceptable business practices. By the turn of the century blatant unethical practices (slavery, child labor), conflicts of interest and monopolistic practices, all of which were considered routine in the early 1800s, were routinely criticized and eventually outlawed.

The contemporary business ethics movement rests on this historical foundation. If it is a fad, it's the longest-running fad ever.

The recent attention being focused on business ethics cannot be dismissed as a superficial managerial "flavor of the month." Its roots are too deep. If we return to the 1970s, to the founding of the Center for Business Ethics and to the beginnings of the modern business ethics movement, we can perhaps better appreciate the extent to which business ethics is linked to important historical events, philosophical movements and cultural trends that have helped shaped our era.

Historians will long note the major changes in the national psyche that occurred in the 1960s and early 70s. Polls tell part of the story. In 1968, 70 percent of Americans believed business tried to strike a balance between profits and the public interest; ten years later only 15 percent believed this was so. Another poll taken for the Center for Business Ethics' First National Conference in 1977 found that big business was rapidly becoming, according to public opinion, the greatest threat to the country's future — a view that had doubled in just ten years.

What caused these major shifts in public opinion? One could certainly point to the Watergate scandal that led to the downfall of President Richard Nixon in 1974 and to the subsequent revelations of illegal campaign contributions and bribery payments by U.S. corporations. One could also point to the Vietnam War and the countercultural revolts of the 1960s that certainly encouraged a strong anti-establishment and anti-business climate. This growing cynicism was fueled by the well-publicized Pinto case, the billion-dollar insurance fraud at Equity Funding, reports of widespread international bribery leading to the Foreign Corrupt

Practices Act, and other business ethics cases. But in addition to these historical causes, there were also four significant philosophical movements that had been influencing the world of ideas for decades and which eventually surfaced movements that became popular in the 60s, 70s and 80s.

Our century has been weaned on four key and interrelated philosophical movements:

- Relativism — the denial of ethical absolutes
- Pragmatism — the belief that something is right if it works
- Positivism — the process of equating of knowledge with observable experience
- Behaviorism — the interpretation of human actions as totally determined and predictable

The thread unifying these four approaches is the reduction of everything considered true and meaningful to material reality — what is tangible and measurable. It is easy to see why science and materialism have flourished in this framework, but ethics and values have been relegated to the realm of emotion, attitude, and feeling — certainly second-class status.

Consider how the four philosophical movements have shaped our popular discourse. How often do we hear discussions about ethical issues — whether on talk shows or over kitchen tables — degenerate suddenly into the modern day mantra: "Oh, well, it's all just a matter of opinion anyway" (relativism)? We're told that "what is important is not what is right or wrong, since no one can say; what is important is what we personally feel" (relativism and positivism).

As the verbal exchange continues, it is often assumed that our behavior, especially our misbehavior, "is not our fault but rather the product of our environment and our genes" (behaviorism). Inevitably, the session's conclusion is a round of practical advice about what will work to fix the problem, with scant attention paid not to whether the solution is right but only to whether it will work. The idea is to "just get it done" (pragmatism).

In addition to *de*valuing freedom, morality, spirituality, and the other nonmaterial, nonmeasurable dimensions of our lives, this world view also has the effect of making the individual the be-all and the end-all. If ethics is only opinion and if all that matters is feeling good and finding a solution that works for you, then you, your opinions and feelings become all-important. Feelings and ego issues become the substitute for serious ethical reflection and discussion.

There is something about the human spirit that resists this sterile and self-centered picture, however. Today, more and more people are searching for a different ideology, one that will preserve our humanity, reconnect us as a community, and provide our lives with value. There is a growing sense of urgency and a recognition that the four philosophic approaches that have dominated our century have left us morally adrift. Business ethics, far from being simply the latest managerial fad, is arising out of the moral crisis created by our century's inadequate philosophies. Business ethics is an attempt, at least in part, to revive the importance and legitimacy of making moral claims in the world of practical affairs.

Myth #3

Ethics is entirely a personal matter. Employees are either ethical individuals or they are not. An organization can't have ethics.

Far too often, on the grounds that ethics is just an individual matter of personal integrity, organizations have failed to take the necessary steps to build an ethical environment. It's assumed that hiring good people will result in having a good company. It's also assumed that corporate wrongdoing happens because certain individuals—"bad apples"—commit wrongful acts; hence we should focus our attention on developing individual integrity, which will then lead to corporate integrity.

There is some truth to these claims. Organizations act on the basis of decisions made by individuals and cannot be ethical unless the people who comprise them are ethical. This position, however, overlooks the essential dynamics between individuals and organizations. Individuals do not operate in a vacuum. Just as organizations are made up of individuals, individuals are dependent on organizations. Individuals gain meaning, direction, and purpose by belonging to and acting out of organizations. Individuals are part of social cultures that are formed around common goals, shared beliefs, and collective duties. As philosopher John Dewey has put it, "apart from ties which bind [the individual] to others, [the individual] is nothing."

The organization can and does influence individual decisions and actions. Each one has its own social culture and character, which, depending on goals, policies, structures and strategies, can exercise good or bad influences. This is underscored by several polls that have shown that a majority of managers of major corporations feel pressure to sacrifice their own personal ethical integrity for corporate goals. For this reason business ethics must direct its attention to issues of *institutional integrity* as as well individual integrity.

We have witnessed outbreaks of business wrongdoing not because business people are less ethical than others, but because business has given too little thought to the issue of developing moral organizations within which individuals can act ethically. Causes of unethical actions are quite often systemic and not simply the result of rotten apples in the corporate barrel. Ethical people can be brought down by serving in a bad organization, just as people with questionable ethical integrity can be uplifted or at least held in check by serving in a good one.

The following tales can help organizations examine their own structures, reporting lines, incentive plans, mission statements, and the largely unspoken—but extremely important—"accepted way of doing things." We hope these stories will help businesses discover **the ethical edge** so that they can begin to take the necessary steps to build organizations that are ready for the opportunities and challenges that lie ahead.

But before we go on to the tales, test your own ethical awareness by taking our quick quiz. We'll be surprised if you score anything less than an "A". Then see how you do when confronted with an ethical decision. Do you know what questions to ask?

2

Quiz Yourself on Business Ethics

We now know that business leaders must consider the impact of their decisions not only on the bottom line but also on others with no direct commercial relation to the decision but who are nevertheless affected by it. How do they balance the sometimes conflicting demands that result? How do they go about making ethical business decisions in the workplace? Can an organization really have a common set of values and a standard for ethical behavior? What should your company be doing to help you make the tough calls?

Answering these questions starts with examining your own ethical awareness as a first step in sorting through issues that remain confusing despite much talk about ethics in recent years. After taking our Ethical Edge 101 quiz, we give our clear, straightforward answers, with commentary, on page 26.

For questions 1 and 2, circle the answers you think are correct. More than one may qualify.

1. **Ethics is** _____

    a. A branch of philosophy that deals with values as they relate to human conduct.

    b. The study of what is good and right for people. It asks the question: How should I act, especially when my actions directly or indirectly affect others?

    c. A fad, a topic that is kept alive by the media on days when there is no hard news to report.

2. **Business ethics is** _____

    a. The application of ethical principles and methods of analysis to business.

    b. A topic of study that is now required at all business schools accredited by the American Assembly of Collegiate Schools of Business.

    c. An oxymoron.

In recent years there have been many tales of moral crises faced by organizations. How many of the following do you recognize? Again, more than one answer may be correct.

3. **Fraud and abuse was so common at NORTEL, Ltd. a giant Canadian telecommunications corporation, that:**

    a. It was estimated that one indictable offense occurred each and every working day.

    b. One manger defrauded the company for more than $6 million and then used the company's facilities to engage in widespread wiretapping, all the while amassing a private stockpile of arms.

   c.   The company has since established a remarkably effective fraud prevention program and is emerging as a leader in the Canadian business ethics movement.

4. **For 15 minutes, executives at the Maine shipbuilder Bath Iron Works gave in to the temptation to cheat. Their ethical lapse:**

   a.   Nearly destroyed the company's 100-year-old reputation for integrity.

   b.   Put 8,000 jobs in peril.

   c.   Ended the gubernatorial aspirations of the company's widely admired leader.

   d.   Pushed the company to establish safeguards at the board and officer levels to increase ethical oversight at the top.

5. **A former president of the United Way was:**

   a.   An entrepreneur and business genius who created the "greatest health and human services delivery system in history."

   b.   A flawed leader who misused United Way funds to support a long-distance romance with a young woman just out of high school.

   c.   Both of the above; in fact his successes helped shape an organization that all but made his failures inevitable.

What do business leaders think about the ethics of business? Deloitte & Touche surveyed more than a thousand officers and directors of corporations together with other business leaders.

Are your views on the topic in sync with theirs? Circle the answers
to questions 6 through 8 that you think are correct.

6. Is the American business community troubled by ethical
    problems?
    a.   Yes
    b.   No

7. Has the issue of business ethics become overblown?
    a.   Yes
    b.   No

8. How do high ethical standards affect a company's competi-
    tive position?
    a.   Strengthen
    b.   Weaken
    c.   No effect

Has the increased acceptance of the concept of business ethics
translated into actual changes in the workplace? In the years 1985,
1990 and 1992, the Center for Business Ethics surveyed the Fortune
1000 to find out what changes—if any—were being made to
build ethics into corporate policies and programs. Circle the
answers you think are correct for questions 9 though 13.

9. What percentage of the Fortune 1000 are planning to expand
    efforts to incorporate ethics into their daily operations?
    a.   More than 90 percent
    b.   About 50 percent
    c.   Less than 25 percent

10. **The most common motive(s) given for implementing ethics initiatives is (are) to:**

    a.   Improve profits

    b.   Provide guidelines for conduct

    c.   Improve public image

    d.   Be socially responsible

11. **What percentage of the Fortune 1000 have written ethics policies?**

    a.   More than 90 percent

    b.   About 50 percent

    c.   Less than 25 percent

12. **What percentage of the Fortune 1000 have employee ethics training?**

    a.   More than 90 percent

    b.   About 50 percent

    c.   Less than 25 percent

13. **Since 1987, the number of large corporations with ethics officers (whose primary function is to create or maintain the company's ethics program) has:**

    a.   Stayed about the same

    b.   Increased slightly

    c.   More than doubled

While there has been a decade of steady growth in the number of corporations implementing corporate ethics policies and programs, the new Federal Sentencing Guidelines for Organizations has certainly piqued the business community's interest and led to a sharp increase in its efforts. Circle the answers you think are correct for questions 14 through 16. More than one answer may be correct.

14. The Guidelines apply only to large corporations.
    a.   True
    b.   False

15. Under the Guidelines organizations may be required to pay restitution and may be placed on probation for up to five years. The Guidelines also cite specific aggravating factors that can increase the organization's fine up to:
    a.   400 percent
    b.   100 percent
    c.   50 percent

16. The Guidelines call on organizations to create "effective programs to prevent and detect violations of law." These programs must include:
    a.   Established compliance standards.
    b.   Specific individual(s) assigned to oversee compliance.
    c.   Due care in delegating discretionary authority.
    d.   Steps to communicate standards and procedures, e.g., training programs and publications.
    e.   Steps to achieve compliance, e.g., monitoring, auditing and reporting systems.
    f.   A record of consistent enforcement of standards.
    g.   Procedures to review and modify the program after an offense.

Hopefully your company is one of those making a serious effort to build ethics into its daily operations. When an ethics dilemma arises, it's unfortunately often the case that, at least initially, you're still facing it alone. What should you do? Circle the answers you think are correct for questions 17 through 20. More than one may be correct.

17. Possible scenarios: (1) **You are an employee at a public utility and discover that rate payers' money is being used illegally to finance political campaigns. (2) You are an employee at a phone company that holds "pervert conventions" every year to "entertain" suppliers. (3) You have a choice of blowing the whistle to your company's officers and possibly facing retaliation or of going outside the company and blowing the whistle to the government and collecting a multimillion-dollar bonus.**

    When faced with such ethical dilemmas, which of the following questions should you ask yourself?

    a.   Have I looked at the problem from the perspective of all the affected parties? Whose interests have priority?

    b.   Who will be harmed and who will be helped? Is there an alternative course of action that will minimize harm?

    c.   If I act unethically, can I get away with it?

    d.   Am I confident that my decision will seem as reasonable over a long period of time as it does now?

    e.   Would I be willing to disclose my decision to my boss, the board, the general public, my family?

18. **If the dilemma is still unresolved, you should:**

    a.   Consult your company's written ethics policies.

    b.   Use your company's hotline or helpline.

    c.   Talk to your company's ethics officer or ombudsman.

    d.   Call your mother.

19. **What companies have faced moral crises, learned their lessons, and now serve as models for how to integrate ethics into their organizations?**

The Business Ethics Quiz — Answers

Question 1

The study of ethics is at least five thousand years old, and ethics was first explicitly applied to business in the Code of Hammurabi around BC 2100. If it's a fad, it's the longest one ever. Reread Myth #2. A and B are correct.

Question 2

A and B are correct. If you answered C, you're out of date. Businesses that ignore ethics are businesses at risk. Reread Myth #1.

Questions 3–5

For each, all of the answers are correct.

Questions 6–8

According to the Deloitte & Touche Survey, 94 percent of the business leaders thought the American business community was troubled by ethical problems, only 32 percent thought the issue was overblown, and 63 percent thought high ethical standards strengthened competitiveness.

Questions 9–13

According to the Center for Business Ethics 1990 survey, more than 90 percent of the Fortune 1000 are planning to increase their business ethics efforts. Their principle motives were to provide guidelines for employee conduct and to be socially responsible (about 95 percent each). Only 43 percent said they were doing so to improve public image, and only 30 percent said they were motivated by profit. More than 90 percent of the Fortune 1000 have written ethics policies, and about 50 percent offer ethics training to employees. According to the Center for Business Ethics' Ethics Officer Survey of the Fortune 1000, the number of large corporations with ethics officers has more than doubled since 1987.

Questions 14–16

The Guidelines apply to business organizations of all sizes including those as small as 10 employees. They also apply to unions, governments and political subdivisions, and nonprofit organizations. If there is high-level complicity, a prior record of the same offense and obstruction of the investigation, the organization's fine could increase 400 percent above the stipulated base fine. The Guidelines call for an "effective program" that includes all of the listed components. Having such a program can reduce an organization's fine by up to 60 percent.

Question 17

If you answered C, go to jail, go directly to jail, do not pass Go, and take this book with you!

Question 18

All four answers are correct. Answers A through C are the standard steps under any "effective program." Answer D is not required under the Guidelines, but it wouldn't hurt to call your mother more often, would it?

Question 19

A hint: They include one of the "baby bells," a giant in the defense industry, and, for the rest, read on in *The Ethical Edge.*

3

How Do You Make Ethical Business Decisions?

We now know that business and ethics do and *must* mix. The question is, how do we go about making ethical business decisions? We believe two steps need to be taken:

- First, managers must develop skills that will enable them to assume what may be called the "ethical point of view."

- Second, corporations must implement ethics policies that include structural and policy supports. These support systems are designed to alleviate unreasonable pressures sometimes put on good people who would not otherwise sacrifice their integrity.

  Sometimes the way to make a decision is to start with questions:

- Have I looked at the problem from the perspective of all the affected parties?

- Who will be harmed and who will be helped?

- Can I discuss the problem with the affected parties before the decision is made?

The Ethical Point of View

How is the ethical point of view attained? Too often we are forced by deadlines and other pressures to look at a problem and simply ask, "How can I resolve this in the most time-efficient way? Questions about long-term consequences, about the direct and indirect effects of the decision on others, and about whether the decision squares with one's own sense of fairness and propriety are too often set aside. When we assume the ethical point of view, we broaden our perspective beyond the immediacy of problem resolution.

- What alternative courses of action do I have?
- Which outcomes are consistent with my values and duties?
- Would I be willing to disclose the decision to my boss, the CEO, the board, my family?
- If someone I respected asked my advice in a similar circumstance, what would I say?
- Could I defend the decision if it were made public?
- What kind of results can I expect if the decision sets a precedent and becomes the general rule?
- Am I confident that my decision will seem as reasonable over a long period of time as it seems now?

The employee who is on the spot is in the best position to ask these questions and to make an initial decision as to whether others need to be brought into the decision-making process. Where the ethical course of action is clear, employees must be certain that they will be supported if they choose to do what they know to be right. Where the ethical course of action is not clear, there must be structural and policy supports within the organization to help the individual employee arrive at an appropriate ethical decision. In all cases, when the employee takes the ethical point of view, he or she needs the support of an ethical corporate culture.

Asking questions is a first step toward making ethical decisions. Developing a strategy for implementing an ethics policy comes next. Different industries and different organizations face different dilemmas, so there is not just one right way to do it. Regardless of form, though, two steps need to be taken:

- The development of the ethical point of view.
- The implementation of a corporate ethics policy.

The goal of the business ethics movement is to encourage organizations to build their own programs for implementing these two steps. Having taken them, the groundwork is laid to better anticipate and appropriately deal with ethically sensitive issues.

Section Two presents tales of organizations that have done it, and the nuts and bolts of how they got started.

What It's All About...
Individual integrity alone is not enough.
Institutional integrity is also essential.

SECTION TWO

AFTER THE "BIG BANG"
RECOVERING A TRADITION AND BUILDING AN ETHICAL CULTURE

4 **NYNEX Corporation**
The "Party Line" Is History

5 **Bath Iron Works**
Fifteen Fateful Minutes

6 **And More "Big Bangs"**
Prudential Securities and National Health Labs

7 **Writing a Code of Ethics**
How to Begin, What to Include

8 **From the Grass Roots**
Tell It Like It Is

9 **So You Think You Need an Ethics Officer**

10 **"You Mean, I'm Going to Jail?!"**
All About the U.S. Sentencing Guidelines

NYNEX Corporation
The "Party Line" Is History

NYNEX, Ethics, and the Information Revolution

The telecommunications, entertainment and computer industries are currently undergoing a period of historic change — one rich in new opportunities as well as unprecedented challenges. Technological advances have taken us to the brink of an information revolution that promises to change not only the way we communicate but also the way we work, the way we learn, and the way we spend our leisure time. The business world has responded to these technological advances and their resultant regulatory changes with a mind-numbing series of mega-mergers and corporate transformations.

The early 90s were a time of reengineering, especially in telecommunications. Flatter organizations were created, and, though profits were up, layoffs were nevertheless widespread. Now, like a Paul Bunyanesque square dance, corporate giants have begun pairing up, switching partners, then swinging this way and that. Among the most energetic dancers are Disney, Microsoft, Time

Warner, Westinghouse, TCI, Intel, Viacom, News Corp., Seagrams, Sony, ABC/Capitol Cities, Turner Broadcasting, General Electric, IBM, Lotus, and the list goes on. With every do-si-do and promenade, the economic landscape rumbled and shook.

Will the changes result in more competition, more innovation and better services for customers? Or less competition, skyrocketing prices and new monopolies? It depends on whom you ask. No one, however, will deny that the stakes are high in this information revolution. One hundred years ago the public debated the wisdom of industrialization policies. The commodities in question at that time were material: oil and steel. Now, as we approach the 21st century, the commodities at issue are less tangible but more important.

The information revolution is all about the creation, control, and distribution of ideas and images. Who will own and control newspapers, magazines, networks, music and film studios, cable franchises, TV and radio stations, on-line services and software manufacturers? How will information, ideas and images be delivered to us, and who will create and control their content? During the last decade we've seen—especially among the MTV generation—the power of the media and entertainment industry to affect both the form and content of political debate. They have altered the way consumers view themselves and the world around them. The stakes are high. The information revolution will have an effect on how we think as well as on what we think about.

Larry Ellison, president and CEO of Oracle Corporation, has said, "The sheer impact of this revolution will rival that of the electric light, the telephone, or, perhaps, printing itself. We won't just talk or shop on the information highway; we will live on it. In twenty years our world will be so transformed by this highway that people will scarcely be able to remember what life was like before it."

Given the high stakes, it's important that corporate players have a clear sense of values, a commitment to public service, and an understanding of the importance of ethics. Unfortunately, two of the three industries involved in this revolution are among the laggards—ethically speaking. With a few notable exceptions (Digital Equipment and Texas Instruments, for example), the computer and entertainment industries have done little in the area of organizational ethics. Fortunately, however, the third industry in this revolution, telecommunications, has been a leader in business ethics. And no telecommunications company has done more in this area than NYNEX.

NYNEX, and the Bell companies in general, have held a long-standing commitment to business ethics. In the 1960s, they were among the first companies to issue corporate codes of ethics. It took a series of unusual events in the 1980s, though, to push NYNEX, and other industry leaders, to a higher standard.

Difficult Times, 1984–1990

The 1984 court-ordered divestiture of AT&T was the beginning of six difficult years for NYNEX. Following divestiture, NYNEX and the other regional Bell companies found themselves in a strange new world. They had to learn to cope with a host of changing rules and regulations being created to deal with the new environment. Customers and markets that were once familiar and

established were gone. In their place was a new competitive industry that was about to get more competitive than anyone at the
time could even dream of.

The external changes triggered a cultural upheaval for
NYNEX's employees. Change is always unsettling, and this was
change on a massive scale. Craig Dreilinger, a business ethics consultant who has helped many companies deal with change, has
noted that there are significant problems that organizations must
cope with when they are going through change. None, he says, is
more potentially damaging than the growth of cynicism.

Cynicism greatly increases during periods of ambiguity. With
change, it's to be expected that some employees will begin to lose
trust in their organizations, their managers, and even their colleagues. Under these conditions, the cynic thrives. In what they
perceive to be a self-serving and selfish environment, the cynics
withdraw their commitment to everything except looking out for
"Number One." Their bad attitude spreads. They assume that
others are as selfish as they are, and they are sure that no one is to
be trusted. In the worst cases, their cynicism can begin to become
a self-fulfilling prophesy.

Dreilinger has listed the most common complaints of the
cynic:

- "Everybody but me seems to benefit from my hard work."
- "Management can't be trusted."
- "The company really doesn't care about 'us.'"
- "Work is just a 'rat race.'"

The complaints of the cynic are part of a vicious cycle.
Change breeds cynicism, cynics spread their beliefs, and their

beliefs make it difficult for the organization to cope with change. NYNEX in the mid-1980's understood this human dynamic and its executives tried to break the cycle.

Then on August 6, 1989, things got worse. All of NYNEX's union-represented employees began a bitter 17-week strike that further polarized the organization. The main issue was health care, but, as is often the case, the strike brought to light other problems that had been just below the surface.

As the strike was ending, NYNEX announced a $43.7 million loss in the fourth quarter of 1989, the first ever for one of the "baby bells." At about the same time, accusations of rate-payer overcharges began to surface.

A few months later, things went from bad to worse. During the summer of 1990, NYNEX's New York Telephone unit was trying to gain approval from the New York State Public Service Commission for a $1.4 billion rate increase. The average consumer's bill would rise 36 percent. In contrast the State Consumer Protection Board was calling for a half-billion-dollar rate *decrease.*

The state attorney general said he would oppose raising rates "even one red cent." His reason? Along with the Public Service Commission, his office was investigating reports that a NYNEX subsidiary hosted suppliers at what the press dubbed "pervert conventions" from 1984 to 1988. In the view of the attorney general's office, "It looks like purchasing was made not on the basis of least cost or best product, but on personal connections and favoritism." It was suspected that NYNEX was now trying to pass on the increased costs to rate payers.

The morning the story of the "conventions" broke, NYNEX

stock fell to $77 per share, down $2.75 from the previous day's close. The more the press and investigators dug, the worse it seemed to be for NYNEX.

"Employee/Vendor Improprieties" (or the "Pervert Conventions")

Following the divestiture of AT&T, NYNEX created a subsidiary to consolidate and gain cost-efficient purchasing for its telephone subsidiaries. Savings would come from the increased scale of purchasing. The purchasing unit, Material Enterprises Company (MECO), provided New York Telephone more than $1 billion annually in equipment and services. Lawrence Friedman was MECO's vice president of purchasing.

What looked like a simple corporate reorganization turned into a controversy as allegations arose that MECO was purposefully created as an unregulated subsidiary in order to avoid scrutiny and as a way of increasing profits to the parent company.

First, as an unregulated subsidiary, MECO could earn profits in excess of those allowed to regulated companies. Second, under regulations, New York Telephone's profits were limited to a certain return on investments. The base for calculating the allowed profit included the company's costs. As costs rose, so too could its allowed profits. From early on there were allegations that MECO was inflating the costs it was charging New York Telephone, thus, in theory at least, increasing the allowable profit for New York Telephone and for NYNEX, its parent company.

These allegations were seemingly later supported by a 1990 audit conducted by the Federal Communications Commission (FCC). The audit determined that between 1984 and 1988 MECO overcharged the telephone companies $118.5 million. (To put this in perspective, if correct, the overcharges represent about 3 percent of the $3.1 billion in total purchases made by MECO between 1984 and 1988.)

Allegations of inflated costs and other improprieties at MECO first surfaced in 1985. At that time it was alleged that Lawrence Friedman was part-owner of a company doing business with MECO, and NYNEX hired an outside law firm to investigate the allegations. The investigation showed that the allegation was false. It further concluded that no ethical or legal problems existed between MECO and its suppliers. Because there was no evidence that NYNEX's code of conduct had been violated, the findings of the investigation were not turned over to authorities.

Unfortunately, however, the 1985 investigation did not go far enough. As William Ferguson, former chairman of NYNEX, later said, "Do I wish the investigation had gone further? Of course I do." If they had pushed further, investigators might have discovered the "pervert conventions" early on, before they got completely out of hand.

Beginning in 1984, MECO employees began gathering annually at the Florida home of a friend of Friedman. The "conventions" grew, under the direction of Friedman, to as many as 100 people, among them MECO and NYNEX employees and suppliers. The "conventions" included initiation rites in which newcomers were thrown into the nearby canal. According to one investigator, "it was grown men making fools of themselves ... getting plastered and then lying on the beach." Female strippers and prostitutes were reportedly hired to provide entertainment and sex for the attendees. Annual "convention" citations were even given out: the Procurement Award for "arranging for women," the Most Valuable Pervert Award, and the Moon Over Miami Award. Friedman assigned hotel rooms so that NYNEX employees would be paired with suppliers apparently to give suppliers an opportunity to pay for the NYNEX employees' expenses.

One former NYNEX employee later said that the Florida "conventions" were a "little window on a larger panorama of procurement abuse, and it's the big picture that has cost New York Telephone rate payers...." Attendance at the "conventions" allegedly resulted in favoritism in contract awards. According to one source, vendors who attended the "conventions" had sales gains with MECO of 67 percent. Those who did not attend had increases of only about 3.5 percent.

The company has said all along that there was no correlation between the "conventions" and vendor favoritism or rate-payer harm. They steadfastly believe that when all the facts are reviewed, they will be exonerated. In 1991, the New York Public Service Commission retained an independent auditor to review New York Telephone's transactions with all of its affiliates between 1984 and 1990. By mid-1995, the final audit report had not yet been released.

The 1985 investigation uncovered nothing. A second investigation, in 1988, was more thorough. It determined that eight employees had violated NYNEX's code of business conduct, which prohibited meetings with suppliers that could be construed as conflicts of interest. In July 1988, Friedman and a supervisor who reported to him were fired. Former NYNEX Chairman Ferguson explained the firings by saying: "The appearance of somebody in a purchasing position going away [to] party with suppliers is not what we can stand, not what we want, and not in keeping with our code of ethics."

Unlike the findings of the 1985 investigation, the 1988 findings were turned over to the Public Service Commission and to the FCC. In addition, Ferguson announced a corporate reorganization that was designed to bring MECO under regulatory scrutiny. He also expressed concerns that employees who were aware of the wrongdoing apparently didn't feel safe enough to report what they knew. Lastly, Ferguson asked for a study of the problem and a review of NYNEX's internal reporting and auditing systems.

At this point, Ferguson could have tried to rationalize the problem as a "perception problem": a good company that was being unfairly berated by the press because of a few "bad apples." He also could have given a speech highlighting the positive steps he had taken, extolling the NYNEX code of conduct and values, and promising to be more vigilant. Had he done all this, everyone would probably have accepted it and applauded him.

But, instead, he went much further. And in so doing he put in motion an ethics process at NYNEX that continues today. It has carried NYNEX to a higher standard and created a model for others to emulate.

The NYNEX Ethics Process

One of Ferguson's first steps was to announce the creation of NYNEX's Office of Ethics and Business Conduct and to name Graydon Wood, a 30-year NYNEX veteran, as vice president of business conduct. Wood would be responsible for setting objectives, developing and directing ethics programs, and providing oversight and counsel to business unit ethics officers. He would report directly to Ferguson and also to the Audit Committee of the Board of Directors. In addition to Wood, NYNEX's initial commitment to ethics included three other managers and a staff of a dozen professionals.

Ferguson also established an Ethics Policy Committee made up of officers from various NYNEX business units. This committee served in an advisory capacity to Ferguson and Wood.

The Office of Ethics and Business Conduct (OE&BC) hit the ground running. It began by benchmarking with General Dynamics, Texas Instruments, United Technologies, and other corporations that had already established ethics initiatives. From the very beginning Wood and his staff understood the importance of three key principles that they would need to follow:

- Maintain the support of senior management and the Board of Directors
- Integrate the ethics initiatives into day-to-day operations and business planning
- Work continually to earn the trust of all employees

The stated objectives of NYNEX's ethics process were to:

- Reinforce and, when necessary, to establish clear, consistent standards of ethical behavior for the entire company
- Develop and maintain an employee body that is aware of ethical issues and educated in ethical decision making and ethical practices
- Provide a formal, confidential channel for reporting possible

wrongdoing and for employee inquiries about the code, policies, regulations, and interpretations

- Communicate continually to all employees about the ethical issues they may face from day to day

- Promote ongoing discussions with employees about their concerns

- Ensure that all standards are applied consistently throughout the organization

With these principles and objectives in mind, over the next two years, from 1990 to 1992, OE&BC accomplished the following:

- Created a single corporate ethics code for all of NYNEX. The NYNEX Code of Business Conduct was drafted by OE&BC and was then reviewed by a cross section of managers.

- Opened and trained the staff of business unit ethics offices throughout the corporation. The staff received training in the corporate ombudsman role, ethics, equal employment opportunity, and sexual harassment, as well as listening and coaching skills.

- Conducted a Values and Vulnerabilities Assessment (VVA) to ascertain operating values, culture, ethical issues, and potential areas of vulnerability. The VVA consisted of interviews with 96 executives and senior managers, 22 focus groups with mid- and lower-level managers, and a survey of a 7,000-member a cross section of employees.

- Established "GuideLines"—telephone numbers and mailboxes for employees to use to ask questions and report possible wrongdoing.

- Began regular publication of the *Ethics Leadership Review,* an internal newsletter focusing on tough ethics issues and possible ways of resolving them.

- Developed and delivered workshops for senior managers. These were designed to increase participants' awareness of ethics issues as perceived by employees, and to give them the necessary skills to ensure that ethical standards are met. Workshops begun for middle managers featured a review of the new Code of Business Conduct and gave participants an opportunity to comment on the draft and on other ethics initiatives.

- Developed and delivered ethics awareness training to 80,000 employees.

- Communicated to all vendors NYNEX's policies on gifts and gratuities and surveyed them to see how they viewed NYNEX's ethical behavior.

Since the beginning of the ethics initiative at NYNEX in 1990, the OE&BC has periodically surveyed managers to assess their understanding and acceptance of the ethics process; to measure improvement, if any, since 1990; and to obtain specific feedback to improve the programs. In a 1993 survey, 83 percent of the managers labeled the process at least "moderately effective," and the positive response rate was much higher if the manager had undergone ethics training or knew firsthand of an ethics investigation. Also encouraging was the finding that 90 percent said the NYNEX Code of Business Conduct was of use in guiding decisions and actions.

The survey also showed, however, that there was little change over the years when it came to experiencing pressure on the job to act inappropriately and to report misconduct.

In sum, though progress was made on many fronts, there still remains hesitation and mistrust in the system. Other companies have learned that this is by far the toughest obstacle to overcome. The only solution is to continue providing managers and others with firsthand experience of how the reporting and investigatory process actually works. If they come to see it as confidential, efficient, and consistently fair, they are more likely to put their trust in it. One botched investigation, or one case that is perceived to be an example of favoritism (even if it really isn't) will set back the program months or years.

Has the program been a success? It's impossible to know how many scandals never occurred because NYNEX had its ethics initiatives in place. You can't measure a negative. Nor can you be sure if the effort will ever pay for itself in the form of improved morale, better quality, customer service, and increased profitability. It's impossible to measure the effect of intangibles on the bottom line — though that doesn't stop some people from claiming they can do so. On the other hand, organizations like NYNEX have learned first hand the price you pay when wrongdoing happens. And in the light of new increased fines under the U.S. Sentencing Guidelines, it's prudent to build an ethics program and reduce an organization's risk.

NYNEX and others are convinced that ethics programs work for them. Wood believes, "They are a key initiative for building trust with all stakeholders, and trust translates to ultimate market share and business success." In some ways it is like a good HMO. Ethics maintenance improves the health and vitality of good companies. Every element of a sound ethics program works to strengthen companies against preventable "illness," and they help "healthy" companies recover when unpreventable problems do strike.

Since its inception, the NYNEX ethics program has had as one of its key, guiding principles the goal of integrating ethics into day-to-day operations. Toward that goal, in 1993, under the direction of Ann Whelehan, then assistant to the president for values and ethics at New York Telephone, NYNEX became the first company to write an Ethics Business Plan, "Putting Values Into Action." It lays out the goals, strategies, initiatives, and methods of measuring success at NYNEX for the 1994–96 period.

Every organization committed to ethics needs to plan for its implementation. Depending on the organization's culture this can be done formally or informally. For most large companies a formal, written plan is best. According to Whelehan, "A plan integrates values into the organization in strategic and practical ways. It also builds teamwork, alignment and commitment." And so, as a model, a summary of the NYNEX Ethics Business Plan follows for the next three pages.

NYNEX ETHICS
BUSINESS PLAN 1994–1996

VISION

Our vision of a NYNEX ethical work environment is one where quality, ethics and caring for the individual are the core values which guide all decisions, actions and behaviors. These values define our reputation in the marketplace and provide the foundation for all interactions with our stakeholders.

MISSION

Our mission is to provide leadership and support that enables NYNEX people to live our core values and Winning Ways behaviors, forstering ethical decision-making through consistent standards, education, communication and guidance.

NYNEX VALUES

- **Quality** — satisfying each customer through sustained excellent performance.
- **Ethics** — living up to the letter and spirit of the law, and our highest expectations for ourselves.
- **Caring for the Individual** — treating individuals as we wish to be treated: with respect for their rights and ideas, and compassion for their needs.

NYNEX WINNING WAYS GUIDING BEHAVIORS

Leadership

Integrity

Accountability

Communications

Teamwork

Employee Involvement

Diversity

Positive Attitude

Embracing Change

Balanced Perspective

(continues)

GOALS	Continually define, apply and demonstrate our values and ethical standards in the context of a dynamic environment	Foster demonstration by all employees on a day-to-day basis that NYNEX is a values-driven and ethical corporation
STRATEGIES	• Develop employee understanding of the importance of employing values and ethical standards while operating in a dynamic environment. • Foster commitment to the Winning Ways behaviors. • Identify new issues with values and ethical implications. • Position values and ethics as certainty in uncertain times to guide employee actions in the development of the corporation	• Encourage the proactive commitment and involvement of leadership in establishing and demonstrating a values-driven environment at NYNEX. • Create and integrate communications initiatives to improve employee understanding of NYNEX's values and standards. • Promote use of the Guide-Line to coach and guide employees on values and ethics-related issues.
1994 INITIATIVES NYNEX Ethics Business Plan 1994–1996 *(continued)*	• Ensure the integration of values and associated behaviors in training. • Educate key groups on power and benefits of managing through values. • Research, develop and conduct ethics training courses for employees. • Initiate incorporation of values, ethics and business conduct as part of the foundation of all business plans. • Identify areas of high risk, develop support guidelines and implement with key groups. • Ensure the corporation conducts values and ethics risk assessments. • Establish a proactive partnership with the Corporate Culture Organization to promote our core values as guides to all decisions, actions and behaviors. • Jointly with the Corporate Culture Organization develop and implement the Living the Values handbook. • Develop employees' critical thinking skills through design and implementation of an ethical decision making model.	• Coach the leadership team to help them understand the importance of sharing the criteria they used for their decision making. • Develop a focused values and ethics message that will be delivered by the Leadership team. • Implement a communications plan that underpins and strengthens NYNEX's values and standards. • Research and design a vehicle to communicate standards established in ethics cases that have implications for all employees. • Initiate and conduct values and ethics awareness discussions with employee groups. • Research, develop and emplement new approaches to enable employees to use the GuideLine process for coaching and guidance on values and ethics inquiries. • Research and establish a NYNEX-wide, cross-functional and cross-level "Ethics At Work" team.
MEASURES OF SUCCESS	• Surveys/focus groups. • Assess business plans. • Validation of assessment tool.	• GuideLine statistics. • Surveys • Observation of demonstrated action.

Ensure consistent application of standards	Strengthen the public's opinion that NYNEX is a values-driven and ethical corporation to improve our competitive position in the marketplace.	Direct the evolution of the ethics process and structure
• Revise the NYNEX Code of Business Conduct in response to a dynamic environment. • Ensure consistency of approaches and interpretations among the Ethics Offices. • Identify new issues with values and ethical implications.	• Implement a focused, proactive plan, together with the leadership of the corporation, Public Affairs and Corporate Communications, that secures the perception of NYNEX as an ethical corporation. • Develop an evaluation process to assess values and ethics implications of partnerships and alliances.	• Develop a plan for the evolution process/structure. • Position the ethics organization as a strategic partner in the single enterprise organization. • Create a development plan for the staff.
• Revise the Code in light of our shared values and behaviors and the dramatic transformation of our industry. • Position the NYNEX Code of Business Conduct as a key resource to guide ethical decision making. • Develop a systematic process for the sharing by staff directors of ethics cases and trends to ensure consistency of approach and interpretation among the Ethics Offices. • Research, develop and implement a confidential mechanized data base for all Ethics Offices to report cases. • Revise the GuideLine procedures to enhance the documentation and analysis of cases. • Develop ongoing communications initiatives with Human Resources.	• Continue to build and foster relationships with professional ethics organizations and selected "best practices" companies to exchange information and ensure NYNEX's reputation. • Develop media plan with liaison organizations, such as Customer Relations and Media Relations, to champion values and ethics in their messages in order to maintain NYNEX's reputation as a values-driven and ethical corporation. • Develop a data gathering tool and survey to assess stakeholder perception.	• Implement and communicate the structural changes outlined in the business case as part of our effort to develop the ethics function to best serve the corporation. • Design and implement a comprehensive training and development plan to maximize and standardize the role of the staff director position in the ethics offices. • Develop a succession plan in order to maintain and ensure continuity in the ethics offices. • Design and conduct an internal and external peer review process. • Redefine and reposition the Ethics Policy Committee. • Form a series of action teams within the Ethics Organization to focus on key values and ethics areas and provide cross-group leadership and action.
• Product delivery. • Commitment to process. • System delivery.	• Press coverage. • Surveys. • Validation of assessment tool.	• Demonstration of actions. • Implementation. • Product delivery.

NYNEX Today

Following the retirement of Graydon Wood in the fall of 1995, the ethics process at NYNEX continues, now under the leadership of Jacquelyn Gates.

In November of 1994, the OE&BC announced that it would be soliciting comments and suggestions to update the original Code of Business Ethics. Though it was only three years old at the time, NYNEX saw the clear advantages in regularly reviewing and updating its contents. Too few organizations do this. Though nearly all large companies have an ethics code, few review it, and fewer still involve employees from throughout the company in the review process. Laws and regulations change. Ethical sensitivity also evolves. Codes written as recently as five years ago may not discuss sexual harassment, work and family issues, HIV discrimination, management of derivative risk, workplace violence, or e-mail and internet policies.

Gates believes that "the involvement of a wide range of employees in 1991 was a critical factor for success. In revising our standards, we have again involved close to 500 employees from hourly workers, to subject experts, to the most senior management levels." The review process itself, especially if it involves managers and other employees, can be a tremendously effective tool to increase the ethics "buy-in." Again, NYNEX has done it right. Its process is a model for others and it is justifiably proud in its updated 1995 Code of Business Ethics.

A current NYNEX initiative is the "Winning Ways" management process. It was devised as a way to ensure that values and principles of behavior remain a top priority even in the midst of reengineering and rapid change. The goal was to create a new corporate culture that will respect the individuality of employees while simultaneously supporting NYNEX as it faces tumultuous changes in its industry. The NYNEX "Winning Ways" is firmly established on a foundation of core values:

- Quality
- Ethics
- Caring for the Individual

"Focus on Winning Ways" spotlights key behaviors to help achieve excellence in the marketplace. Full text is on page 52.

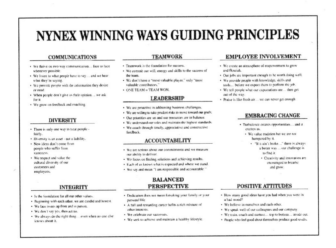

NYNEX WINNING WAYS GUIDING PRINCIPLES

COMMUNICATIONS
- We thrive on two way communication... face to face whenever possible.
- We listen to what people have to say... and we hear what they're saying.
- We provide people with the information they desire or need.
- When people don't give us their opinion... we ask for it.
- We grow on feedback and coaching.

DIVERSITY
- There is only one way to treat people - fairly.
- Diversity is an asset - not a liability.
- New ideas don't come from people who suffer from sameness.
- We respect and value the cultural diversity of our customers and employees.

INTEGRITY
- Is the foundation for all our other values.
- Beginning with each other, we are candid and honest.
- We face issues up front and in person.
- We don't say yes, then act no.
- We always do the right thing ... even when no one else knows about it.

TEAMWORK
- Teamwork is the foundation for success.
- We commit our will, energy and skills to the success of the team.
- We don't have a "most valuable player," only "most valuable contributors."
- ONE TEAM = TEAM WON.

LEADERSHIP
- We are proactive in addressing business challenges.
- We are willing to take prudent risks to move toward our goals.
- Our priorities are set and our resources are in balance.
- We understand our roles and maintain the highest standards.
- We coach through timely, appreciative and constructive feedback.

ACCOUNTABILITY
- We are serious about our commitments and we measure our ability to deliver.
- We focus on finding solutions and achieving results.
- Each of us knows what is expected and where we stand.
- We say and mean "I am responsible and accountable."

BALANCED PERSPECTIVE
- Dedication does not mean forsaking your family or your personal life.
- A full and rewarding career befits a rich mixture of other interests.
- We celebrate our successes.
- We seek to achieve and maintain a healthy lifestyle.

EMPLOYEE INVOLVEMENT
- We create an atmosphere of empowerment to grow and flourish.
- Our jobs are important enough to be worth doing well.
- We provide people with knowledge, skills and tools... before we expect them to perform the job.
- We tell people what our expectations are ... then get out of the way.
- Praise is like fresh air ... we can never get enough.

EMBRACING CHANGE
- Turbulence creates opportunities... and it excites us.
- We value tradition but we are not hampered by it.
- "If it ain't broke ..." there is always a better way ... our challenge is to find it.
- Creativity and innovation are encouraged to breathe and grow.

POSITIVE ATTITUDES
- How many good ideas have you had when you were in a bad mood?
- We believe in ourselves and each other.
- We speak well of our colleagues and our company.
- We train, coach and nurture... top to bottom... inside out.
- People who feel good about themselves produce good results.

NYNEX Winning Ways Guiding Principles

COMMUNICATIONS

- We thrive on two-way communication ... face to face whenever possible.
- We listen to what people have to say ... and we hear what they're saying.
- We provide people with the information they desire or need.
- When people don't give us their opinion ... we ask for it.
- We grow on feedback and coaching.

DIVERSITY

- There is only one way to treat people—fairly.
- Diversity is an asset—not a liability.
- New ideas don't come from people who suffer from sameness.
- We respect and value the cultural diversity of our customers and employees.

INTEGRITY

- Is the foundation for all our other values.
- Beginning with each other, we are candid and honest.
- We face issues up front and in person.
- We don't say yes, then act no.
- We always do the right thing...even when no one else knows about it.

TEAMWORK

- Teamwork is the foundation for success.
- We commit our will, energy and skills to the success of the team.
- We don't have a "most valuable player," only "most valuable contributors."
- ONE TEAM = TEAM WON.

LEADERSHIP

- We are proactive in addressing business challenges.
- We are willing to take prudent risks to move toward our goals.
- Our priorities are set and our resources are in balance.
- We understand our rules and maintain the highest standards.
- We coach through timely, appreciative and constructive feedback.

ACCOUNTABILITY

- We are serious about our commitments and we measure our ability to deliver.
- We focus on finding solutions and achieving results.
- Each of us knows what is expected and where we stand.
- We say and mean "I am responsible and accountable."

BALANCED PERSPECTIVE

- Dedication does not mean forsaking your family or your personal life.
- A full and rewarding career befits a rich mixture of other interests.
- We celebrate our successes.
- We seek to achieve and maintain a healthy lifestyle.

EMPLOYEE INVOLVEMENT

- We create an atmosphere of empowerment to grow and flourish.
- Our jobs are important enough to be worth doing well.
- We provide people with knowledge, skills and tools ... before we expect them to perform the job.
- We tell people what our expectations are...
- Praise is like fresh air...we can never get enough.

EMBRACING CHANGE

- Turbulence creates opportunities...and it excites us.
- We value tradition but we are not hampered by it.
- "If it ain't broke..." there is always a better way...our challenge is to find it.
- Creativity and innovation are encouraged to breathe and grow.

POSITIVE ATTITUDES

- How many good ideas have you had when you were in a bad mood?
- We believe in ourselves and each other.
- We speak well of our colleagues and our company.
- We train, coach and nurture...top to bottom ...inside out.
- People who feel good about themselves produce good results.

5

BATH IRON WORKS
FIFTEEN FATEFUL MINUTES

It was five o'clock on the morning of May 17, 1991. A janitor was cleaning a conference room at the North Stores Conference Center of Bath Iron Works (BIW) when, on a chair, he found a document stamped "Business Sensitive." It turned out to contain 67 pages of sensitive information about one of BIW's competitors. How did the document get there? Had it been left behind intentionally to test the ethics of BIW employees? Was someone trying to create a scandal in order to benefit from the fallout? Or had the document simply been left behind by mistake by a participant at the previous day's meeting with the Navy?

No one would ever know for sure. But the document, and how it was handled, touched off a crisis that put in peril 8,000 jobs, nearly destroyed the company's 100-year-old tradition for integrity, ended the careers of several executives and managers, and destroyed the gubernatorial aspirations of the company's CEO. The incident also played a role in the improvement of an ethics program at Bath Iron Works that was already exceptional. The tale serves as a lesson to us all that, in matters of ethics, we

can never let down our guard. A lot can happen in a fateful 15
minutes.

BIW, the largest employer in Maine, in 1991 was one of only
two shipyards in the country capable of building the nation's next
generation of missile-equipped naval destroyers. In May of that
year it was engaged in a fierce competition for the contract. The
day before that document was found, Navy officials and executives from BIW had met in the conference room as part of a routine review of ships already under construction at the shipyard.
The next morning the janitor made his discovery.

At the start of the business day, the janitor turned the document over to BIW's vice president of finance. Upon examining it,
he found nothing to indicate to whom it belonged. He also saw
that the document contained a comparative analysis of the performance and profitability of BIW and its competitor. This was
clearly proprietary information. He should have known this and
he should have called the Navy immediately. He didn't. What he
did next was the beginning of the near disaster for BIW.

The VP of finance reviewed the data, made notes, then called
in a vice president–director in the Contracts Division. The two
examined the document and decided to take it on to the CEO,
William Haggett. Because Haggett was in a hurry to deliver a luncheon speech, he took only 15 minutes—a fateful 15 minutes—
to review the document. Heading out the door, he told the others
to make a photocopy, return the original to the conference room,
and meet with him when he got back to discuss how to further
handle the situation.

Over the next four hours the two executives continued to

review the information and one of them did some computer modeling based on it. They discussed the matter further over lunch and eventually informed Howard Yates, senior vice president in the Finance and Administrative Group of its existence. Yates was apparently the first one to be troubled by the situation and to recognize the severity of the matter. He immediately called "Buzz" Fitzgerald, the president and COO of the company, and brought him up to date on what had happened.

Fitzgerald was appalled, particularly in light of the steps that BIW had taken to ensure that ethics would be a priority in its corporate culture. BIW's history stretches all the way back to the 1800s, and the company is proud of its traditions and reputation for integrity. But BIW did not just rest on its history. In 1986, the Maine shipbuilder had joined 54 other defense contractors in an unprecedented industrywide voluntary ethics program called the Defense Industry Initiative (DII) on Business Ethics and Conduct.

The Defense Industry Initiative on Business Ethics and Conduct

In the mid-1980s widespread allegations of waste, fraud, and abuse in the defense industry were common, including charges of:

- Falsification of time cards and test results
- Lax quality controls
- Defective pricing
- Overall mismanagement of defense contracts

In July 1985, President Ronald Reagan appointed a commission led by David Packard, chairman of Hewlett-Packard, to recommend a solution to the problems. The Packard Commission concluded that: "To assure that their houses are in order, defense contractors must promulgate and vigilantly enforce codes of ethics that address the unique problems and procedures incident to defense procurement. They must also develop and implement internal controls to monitor these codes of ethics and sensitive aspects of contract compliance."

The Packard Commission report led directly to the creation of the DII. In all, 55 companies voluntarily signed on and agreed to meet the DII standards. The signatories included 22 of the 25 largest defense contractors, and BIW was among the signatory companies.

This was not a public relations ploy. The companies involved were quite obviously hoping that by cleaning up their own houses they would avoid cumbersome new regulations. But they also knew that their efforts would take the pressure off only if they were significant and effective. Consequently, the DII companies agreed to meet the following principles:

- Each company will formulate and adhere to a written code of business ethics and conduct.

- Each company's code will establish high standards that are clear enough to enable employees to judge their own conduct and that of their organization.

- Each company will train their employees concerning their responsibilities under its code.

- Each company will create a free and open atmosphere that allows and encourages employees to report possible violations of its code without fear of retribution.

- Each company will set up methods for monitoring compliance with the code and with regulations.

- Each company will participate in an annual Best Practices Forum to share with other companies programs to improve the level of ethics throughout the industry.

- Each company's compliance with the DII principles will be reviewed by a Board of Directors Committee made up of outside directors.

- Each company will submit an annual report on its compliance with the DII principles to a third party that will then summarize the results for the industry as a whole and release the information to the public.

The Aftermath

Knowing BIW's tradition and the commitments under DII, Fitzgerald knew that steps had to be taken to resolve the problem. He also knew that the stakes were high. Possession of the document might mean that the company and the executives involved were in violation of the Procurement Integrity Act. He knew that this might mean civil penalties of up to $100,000 per person and criminal penalties of up to five years in jail; he knew that BIW could be fined up to $1 million. And, perhaps more ominously, violations could even mean debarment, which would prevent BIW from bidding on government contracts. That would be the end of the company.

Fitzgerald ordered the destruction of the copy and the return of the original document to the Navy. At this point Haggett, the CEO, returned from his luncheon address. He immediately recognized his mistakes in handling the document and personally agreed to hand-deliver the document to the Navy's supervisor of shipbuilding stationed at BIW.

The Navy's Suspension and Debarment Committee reviewed the incident and BIW's response to it. For a while it looked like the company actually would be debarred. Instead, though, in November 1991, a settlement agreement was reached. Haggett, a strong favorite to become Maine's next governor, was asked to resign from the company. The two officers who had first reviewed the document were also asked to leave. Three other employees who had indirectly been made aware of the contents of the document were required to recuse themselves from any further business decisions that might have anything to do with the information.

As part of the settlement, BIW also agreed to board-level and company-level changes that went beyond the DII principles BIW was already following. The changes were to:

Board-level

- Establish a Board Ethics Committee.
- Name three outside directors to the board (there had previously been none).
- Create a board procedure for investigating suspected wrongdoing by company officers.

Company-level

- Establish an internal Ethics Committee.
- Name an ethics officer.
- Expand ethics training.
- Report to the Navy quarterly for three years on investigations and implementation of an ethics program.

In many ways BIW went beyond the requirements of the settlement. While the Navy required that there be three outside directors, BIW named five, including a well respected retired vice admi-
ral who it also named to be the chair of the Board's Ethics
Committee. The Navy called for a three-member company-level
ethics committee, but BIW formed a committee of six members,
in part to ensure that the committee would include a cross section
of employees from throughout the company.

BIW's ethics program is today led by its new CEO, Buzz
Fitzgerald, its Ethics Officer Kevin Gildart, and by Harry Britt,
BIW's director of internal audit. Many elements of the BIW ethics
program, especially its company-level ethics committee and its
ethics office, can serve as models for other organizations.

BIW Company-level Ethics Committee

- The committee is chaired by the ethics officer. Other members are chosen from a broad cross section of the company.

The responsibilities of the committee are to:

- Offer liaison between the Board Ethics Committee and the
  company
- Provide guidance and direction on the development and
  implementation of the ethics program
- Provide direction and guidance to the Ethics Officer
- Review all ethics-related policies and procedures before approval
- Render advice on ethics matters as requested
- Audit and monitor compliance with BIW's standards to assure
  the quality and consistency of the ethics program throughout
  the organization

- Review on a regular basis the ethics officer's disposition of helpline calls, incidents, and investigations
- Approve the disposition of gifts in excess of $25
- Identify topics for ethics training and preview and approve all ethics-related training programs
- Report regularly on the status of ethics programs to the Board Ethics Committee
- Review quarterly status reports prior to submittal to the Navy

BIW Ethics Officer

- BIW's ethics officer reports directly to the president, to the company-level ethics committee, and to the board-level ethics committee;

The duties of the ethics officer are to:

- Prepare recommendations and detailed plans on ethics-related policies and procedures;
- Assist all managers and staff in the maintenance of their ethics efforts and activities;
- Assist divisions in developing and implementing continuous programs for communicating, implementing, and monitoring the status of their ethics programs;
- Ensure that a confidential communications process is maintained that will enable any employee with an ethics-related concern or report of a possible violation to come forward without fear of retaliation or inappropriate exposure;
- Function as an ethics counselor and adviser;

- Develop investigatory and disciplinary procedures for ethics-related matters and ensure that they are in place;
- Serve as chair of the company-level ethics committee;
- Assist other managers, in cooperation with public affairs personnel, in their liaison activities with external audiences, including subcontractors, suppliers, consultants, and academe.

Buzz Fitzgerald and Kevin Gildart are now leaders in the movement to make the principles and programs of a sound business ethics initiative more accessible to all organizations. They know firsthand what a close call BIW had and how little it can take to destroy the trust customers, suppliers, regulators, and citizens have given over the years.

Putting in place an ethics program like BIW's requires months, even years, of effort. A scant 15 minutes can unravel it. So Fitzgerald and Gildart have a mission. They don't need to tell the BIW tale anymore. They'd rather talk about the company's commitment to ethics, which is as it should be. BIW now has **the ethical edge** and is ready to face whatever challenges lie ahead.

6

AND MORE "BIG BANGS"
PRUDENTIAL SECURITIES AND
NATIONAL HEALTH LABORATORIES

NYNEX and Bath Iron Works weren't the first — nor will they be the last — organizations to have undergone an ethical "big bang." The scenario is unfortunately all too common. What sets NYNEX and BIW apart from most is the recovery they've made and the extent to which they've committed themselves to maintaining **the ethical edge.** The same can be said of the companies in our next two tales: Prudential Securities and National Health Laboratories.

After experiencing their own "big bangs," both are now working to restore their traditional values and build an ethical culture. We begin with the story of Prudential Securities.

The Costliest Scandal in Wall Street history

Beginning in 1980, Bache & Co. and Prudential Securities Inc. sold limited partnerships in real estate, oil, gas, and other ventures. In 1981, Prudential acquired Bache & Co. The new corporate entity, Prudential-Bache Securities Inc. (PSI), continued to sell the investment partnerships. Lawyers estimate that throughout the 1980s about 340,000 parties invested $8 billion in the 700 limited partnerships.

Unfortunately for those investors, in 1986 the U.S. Congress passed a Tax Reform Act that closed a loophole allowing a deduction for losses from the partnership investments. Under the new tax law, limited partnerships became less desirable as an investment vehicle. Prudential Insurance Company, the parent company of Prudential-Bache Securities Inc., realized the significance of the change and stopped investing in limited partnerships themselves. PSI, however, continued to sell them.

Customers alleged that brokers used misleading sales tactics to convince some investors, among them retirees, that the limited partnerships were safe and involved only minimum risk, when they in fact suited only wealthy investors. Internal PSI marketing materials described the partnerships as safer than they really were, and brokers got a clear message that their primary objective was increased sales.

One Texas regulator described the scam as "continuous practices of sales abuse and fraud.... In modern times, nothing comes close to it."

Legal action began in 1991 when PSI clients began to file class-action lawsuits. The company initiated its own internal investigations and tried to settle cases. Of the 340,000 original investors, about 200,000 filed claims. PSI paid full or partial compensation to about 100,000 of the claimants, rejecting 25,000 other claims, and deliberating about the rest.

Customers did not limit their accusations of fraud to the limited partnerships. They accused Prudential Securities' brokers of churning accounts, of encouraging high-pressure sales tactics not only with its partnerships but also with its mutual funds, and of allowing an executive who was supervising the limited partnership program to have extensive personal financial dealings with the head of a firm he was supposed to be supervising. Perhaps not surprisingly, the flood of accusations also brought to the surface problems that occurred in the late 70s that could have served as an early warning to PSI, but which were not followed up.

The Root Cause

Jack Casey, a former managing director at the investment firm of Scudder, Stevens & Clark, and later a lecturer, author, and executive fellow at the Center for Business Ethics, described appropriate standards in his *Ethics in the Financial Marketplace:*

"Putting the client's interest first requires a great deal of specific knowledge about how transactions work. Without a grasp of such details, the alternatives cannot be identified.... While principles of self-interest and looking-out-for-the-other-person don't change, the details are constantly changing, especially at the margin. As a result, ethics must come from the managers who process transactions...."

In other words, investors have to be able to trust individuals who invest their money. Stockbrokers, mutual fund managers, financial advisers, and others on and off Wall Street must earn that trust every day. If the folks on Main Street believe that the people on Wall Street can't be counted on to live up to their fiduciary responsibilities, then it won't be long before Main Street will begin to see the investment world as a rigged game. Investors' money will go elsewhere.

Everyone in the financial services industry knows this, but not enough demonstrate this principle in practice. Perhaps it is because money managers also realize that the stakes are higher than ever before. Securities firms face competition from banks, mutual funds, and insurance companies. The financial marketplace has never been more competitive. As the options available to investors increase, trust becomes a critical factor in success or failure; a trusted name can give a company a valuable edge in the marketplace.

Observers of the financial scene may wonder why investment scandals continue to occur so often, given the enormous risks to reputation and viability. The simple answer is greed. But, like everything else, nothing is as simple as it first appears.

Investment scandals, like the other crises we've looked at, can't be easily dismissed as the product of "rotten apples," or in this case, "rogue brokers." Organizations, and even entire industries, help set priorities, establish acceptable levels of conduct, and determine norms of behavior. In the financial marketplace one of the major contributing causes of wrongdoing is the compensation and bonus system used throughout the industry.

Compensation and bonus plans are designed in a way that all but encourages unscrupulous money managers to ignore the best interests of their clients and instead churn accounts and generate sales volume. Many Wall Street firms have been slow to link compensation schemes with meeting the clients' needs, even though there are ways of objectively measuring how well a manager performs in this area.

The Securities and Exchange Commission's Committee on Compensation Practices has put forward recommendations to the industry. Until industrywide standards are accepted, however, it's difficult, if not impossible, for one firm to move out ahead of the pack and change the rules of the game. If a firm tried to do this, its managers would simply resign and go elsewhere. If ever there was a case for an industrywide approach to an ethical problem, this is it.

Until the investment industry addresses its compensation challenges, one thing is sure: The Prudential Securities scandal won't be the last of its kind, although it would take a large one indeed to exceed it in dollar amount. More important than money, though, is the fact that the case tarnished the reputation of the firm, ruined the careers of several executives, and resulted in the government placing the company on probation until 1997.

As part of an October 1994 agreement that enabled the firm to avoid criminal indictment, Prudential Securities admitted criminal wrongdoing and agreed to contribute tens of millions of dollars to a fund that had already been set up for defrauded clients. The additional contribution brought the fund up to $660 million. Under the agreement, if any future wrongdoing occurs at Prudential Securities during the three-year period, the company will face indictment.

The company estimates that the $660 million settlement fund, plus the costs of legal fees and other settlements, will eventually bring the total cost of its fraud to almost $2 billion, making it the most expensive scandal in Wall Street history. Runner-up status goes to the late Drexel Burnham Lambert, Inc., which settled a securities scandal in its junk-bond department for $650 million, less than half of what Prudential Securities will ultimately pay.

Prudential Securities Reborn

All the company's senior executives from the 1980s are gone.

George L. Ball, chief executive from 1982 to 1991, resigned in 1993; Loren Schechter, Prudential Securities general counsel from 1982 through 1993, resigned from the firm in July 1995. A spokesperson for the company underscored the changes: "We're operating as a new Prudential Securities. Our current clients and employees think of us as a company that's different from the way we were in the 1980s.... We have new management, a new philosophy, a new style."

In January 1994, Prudential Securities appointed, as its new corporate ethics officer, Jim Settel, a business ethics professor at Skidmore College. Settel had worked in the securities industry since 1958, including a 15-year association with Prudential as director of corporate training. He also had been a member of the firm's board of directors.

Settel was given wide latitude to shape the ethics officer position. In an interview with the business ethics newsletter *Ethikos,* he explained that one of his first priorities was to "create an integrity strategy." This meant reviewing all of the plans, policies, and products that the firm was putting out. He wanted to review these "from the point of view of the client, both the external client, who is the investor, and the internal client, who is the broker. What were investors being told about the product? What were stockbrokers being told?"

Settel's next step was to visit branch managers. He looked to them for suggestions about potential problem areas, and he left them with the sense that he was a person they could call for answers and to discuss whatever was worrying them. As he told *Ethikos,* "I'm a worrier. I've been a worrier since I was five years old. I tell them it's all right to lay their worries on me, because I'm going to worry anyway."

Clearly Settel is aware that the efforts of the ethics office at Prudential Securities are integral to the company's performance:

"Prudential has long recognized the relationship between ethics and organizational success," says Settel. "Our reputation for honesty and integrity at this firm was earned over many years through the day-to-day decisions of many thousands of Prudential people, past and present. Painfully, we know the consequences when this relationship is not nurtured. The obvious costs of litigation and fines, combined with the loss of good customers, loyal employees, and the wounded pride left in its wake are simply unacceptable."

In June 1994, Settel hired Keith Darcy, a former banking executive and more recently the president of a national ethics and leadership consulting group. Settel gave Darcy the responsibility of leading an all-out effort to deliver ethics training to the company's 17,000 employees.

The new training program at Prudential Securities aims to remove some of the stigma associated with "ethics talk" and tries to make ethical deliberation more acceptable. Darcy explained that he will be training trainers. Branch managers will then pass the training on to brokers, and the message will cascade down to the grass roots.

The training strategy takes a comprehensive approach. Darcy's major initiative has been to design, develop, and deliver the firm's Ethics Awareness Workshop, which will be rolled out across the company. The objectives of the workshop are to

- Raise generate and enhance the awareness of ethical issues in the workplace
- Exercise people's critical thinking skills
- Make employees aware of the ethical implications of their actions
- Raise the awareness of Prudential Securities' resources to assist employees who are faced with a dilemma.

These objectives are accomplished by introducing short, business-specific cases that present important, compelling points of view in conflict with each other. Groups of 25 are broken up into small groups of four or five for case discussion.

According to Darcy, "It's important that ethics not be perceived as something set apart from business, but embedded within daily business operations. Presenting case dilemmas that people face in their day-to-day work, in a highly interactive environment, allows participants to observe a wide range of alternative decisions. From this, they can begin to distinguish better answers from worse."

As part of the rollout strategy, Darcy is training branch managers to facilitate the Ethics Awareness Workshop in their respective offices. "This not only helps us to efficiently reach a large and geographically diverse group, but also places ownership of this initiative squarely in the businesses," says Darcy.

Different cases are developed not only for each business, but also for different positions and functions in those businesses. Additionally, they may be customized according to the level within the organization. As Darcy says, "The more participants can relate to the cases, the more involvement in the workshop and the greater the learning that takes place."

In addition to the Ethics Awareness Workshops, ethics modules have also been developed for new employees, for branch managers, and in the product training area for investment management.

Darcy also observes that the by-product of these sessions is significant. "Team building and a much needed morale boost has been clearly evidenced from these initiatives."

The Client

One of your long-time clients, George, is in his late 50's. In addition to his personal account, you also manage accounts for several large family trusts. Because you've known him for so long, you're familiar with his behavior patterns. Over the past several months you have observed some disturbing lapses in his mental functions. Frequently he is unable to concentrate, seems to be complacent over issues that he was once very concerned about, and is noticeably forgetful.

He called you today to ask you to invest in a very risky bond offering. You tell him about your concerns and specifically say that this investment has too high a level of risk, and is clearly a wrong investment fit for his objectives. He vehemently disagrees and insists you buy the bonds. You...

a. buy the bonds. He has a right to invest in whatever he pleases.

b. fax a letter to him articulating your concerns.

c. tell him you can't execute the buy order until you have received written instructions.

d. contact George's family and explain your concerns.

As part of the firm's comprehensive ethics strategy, Settel has also been actively involved in launching a Credo initiative. This involves facilitating the development of a series of business-specific ethics credos. These credos are based on the firm's Core Values.

In late 1991, Prudential Insurance introduced Core Values, four imperatives guiding the firm's corporate culture and business conduct:

- Worthy of Trust
- Customer Focused
- Respect for Each Other
- Winning

"The universality of these values is both a strength, as well as a weakness," says Settel. "They are broad enough to have meaning across all business units and hierarchies, but because they apply to all, they do not speak specifically to the key points of professional behavior. Creating a credo for our brokers, for example, will help articulate the 'best practices' for their clients, while serving as a natural compliment to our Core Values."

Settel formed a task force comprised of brokers from around the country. Among the representatives were management-nominated brokers who reflected a cross section of individuals who were well known for their high ethical standards. The task force's short-lived mission was to create the initial draft of the credo for the Retail Group. After formulating several iterations, members sent a working draft to brokers in several branches for their critical assessment. This feedback was worked into a draft that was sent to every branch in the Prudential system for similar input. "It is critical for this document to have meaning, that it be created by the practitioners themselves, and not be handed down by management," said Settel. "By following this process, we are creating a practical and realistic code of conduct by each business unit."

While supervising ethical activities within the firm, Settel also recognizes that many of the issues Prudential wrestles with are systemic to the industry. "Although we were the first — and are still the only — major Wall Street firm with an ethics initiative, we cannot be proprietary about our efforts. All of us need all the help we can get if we're going to contribute to setting higher standards for the consuming public," said Settel.

The varied ways in which Settel and Darcy have been involved in industrywide efforts are a clear demonstration of Prudential's commitment to lead the industry. Settel is an active member of the Security Industry Association's (SIA) important Public Trust and Confidence Committee as well as its Education Committee. In that capacity Settel urged the Securities Industry Institute at the University of Pennsylvania's Wharton School of Business to make ethics training a required course. He and Darcy taught the first ethics classes there. Additionally, Settel and Darcy have made numerous presentations at professional ethics conferences not only to let people know about the new initiatives at Prudential Securities, but to be sure that they both remain part of the ongoing dialogue on ethics in the securities industry.

Settel was also the catalyst for the New York Stock Exchange's first-ever Conference on Ethics, which was attended by leaders of the securities industry as well as by the security industry's leading regulators.

Prudential Securities' integrity-based strategy is a long-term plan with special emphasis on individual responsibility for ethical behavior.

Says Settel: "We need to create a climate that strengthens the relationships and reputation of the firm by fostering self-governance. By doing so, we will set an unimpeachable example for the future."

How Healthy Are Your Ethics?

About one trillion dollars is spent annually on health care in America. In 1992, the U.S. General Accounting Office estimated that fraud and deceitful practices may have accounted for between $20 billion and $75 billion. Unfortunately, the higher figure may have been more accurate. Today, it is estimated that nearly 10 percent of the nation's health care budget is being lost to fraud! No wonder investigatory agencies have shifted much of their manpower over the last five years away from chasing spies and have sent their sleuths to work on cleaning up billions of dollars' worth of fraud in the health care industry.

Some of the first targets in this new investigatory focus have included National Health Laboratories, Incorporated (NHL), National Medical Enterprises (NME), Caremark, the Hanlester Network, Smith Kline Clinical Laboratories, and Metpath. Most recently, there have been whistle-blower allegations made against the hospital chain Columbia/HCA.

These NHL, NME, and Caremark investigations have either resulted in settlements, fines, jail sentences or both. In 1992, NHL agreed to pay $111.4 million and its president was sentenced to three months in jail and paid a substantial fine. In the same year, National Medical Enterprises (NME) was sued by ten insurance companies alleging $740 million in fraud. Soon after, 600 federal agents raided the company's headquarters and a three-year investigation ensued. NME ultimately made a $360 million settlement with the government and paid another $215 million to settle charges brought by private insurers and the Securities and Exchange Commission. In the Caremark case, it is alleged that bribes were paid to physicians to refer patients to the company's home health care services network. In 1995 Caremark agreed to pay $161 million in civil and criminal penalties, including $45 million to various state Medicaid funds.

While these settlements are to date the largest in the area of health care fraud, industry critics predict that there are plenty more to come. Some see the situation as being similar to the experience of the defense industry in the 1980s. After several years of investigations and growing public resentment over "waste, fraud, and abuse," the defense industry, with its back against the wall, initiated an industrywide set of ethics and compliance standards. The Defense Industry Initiative (DII), described in Chapter 5, helped for a time to quiet calls for increased regulation of the industry. Today, the DII serves as a model for other industry groups. Should the health care industry adopt a similar approach? Are there industrywide problems that require an industrywide solution? Or is the health care industry different from the defense industry and made up of too many competing interests? To help decide, let's look at the tale of National Health Laboratories.

National Health Laboratories

The NHL story is important not only because it was one of the
first "shots across the bow" of the health care industry, but also
because there is still debate about whether the company's activities were unethical or even strictly illegal. It is also an important
tale because the settlement and ensuing jail sentence of the company's president were clearly intended to send a message to the
rest of the health care industry.

The government's case against NHL centered on the
"bundling" of HDL cholesterol and serum ferritin tests with the
company's commonly ordered tests. The government believed that
the way the tests were "bundled" on NHL test order forms, as well
as the way they were priced, led physicians to order—and government health programs to pay for—a large number of HDL
cholesterol and serum ferritin tests that were not medically necessary. The company argued that both the "bundling" and pricing
policies were common practice in the industry and that all tests
were billed in full compliance with requirements. The government
rejected these arguments, pointing out that in the end, the practices resulted in the ordering of unnecessary procedures.

Legally, NHL's defenders may be on solid ground. Ethically,
the NHL tale may be a case in which a company paid too much
attention to whether or not its practices were "in compliance" and
not enough attention to whether its practices would be perceived
to be ethical.

On the heels of their settlement, the company took immediate steps to develop and expand their ethics and compliance programs. A consulting firm was hired to help identify key compli-

ance risk areas and to administer companywide employee ethics surveys. The board of directors formed an ethics committee that directed the appointment of a chief compliance officer (a senior officer in the company). NHL also hired a former United States attorney as its general counsel to help implement the new program.

Following these initial actions, NHL hired a former federal law enforcement official as its vice president of compliance and security. Together, those serving in these new roles were directed to set a high ethical standard for NHL and, by extension, for the entire clinical laboratory industry. A revised code of conduct for the company was developed, and ethics training of managers, supervisors, sales, and client services personnel was begun.

Part of the NHL program has been the formation of a high-profile compliance audit team. Internal audit standards were revised to improve the company's operating practices and help uncover conditions that could lead to possible wrongdoing.

In addition, a culture of self-disclosure is being encouraged throughout the company. It is openly monitoring its billing and laboratory practices on a regular basis and has made a commitment to cooperate with all government agencies and private third-party payers. Employees have been encouraged to use the company open door policy to solve problems, get answers, raise concerns, and report illegal or improper conduct. They are also encouraged to use the Ethics Action Line when the normal chain of communications does not work, or when the employee fears reprisal or retribution. Additionally, the company has incorporated into its program the position of Division Compliance Officer in each of its divisions nationwide. One role is to ensure that the compliance program is functioning properly at the division level; another role is to design division-level audits to assess areas of risk, both internal and external.

Is this the beginning of a health care industry initiative? Some believe it is, and they sincerely hope it is a first step toward helping this industry gain **the ethical edge.**

7

WRITING A CODE OF ETHICS
HOW TO BEGIN, WHAT TO INCLUDE

We now know that organizations with the most effective ethics programs make use of up-to-date, written codes of ethics. Such codes provides the foundation for the entire ethics initiative by communicating standards and expectations as well as by providing useful information to help employees deal with difficult ethical dilemmas.

Several surveys have shown that more than 95 percent of midsize to large companies have a written code; we have observed that many small businesses and nonprofit organizations are also now instituting their own codes.

What makes an effective, useful code of ethics? We've culled the best elements from the best ones:

A Rose Is a Rose...

No doubt everyone has heard or seen Codes of Values, Codes of Practice, and Compliance Codes. While these variations are similar in many ways, each has its own characteristic style and content.

Code of Values—a set of general statements of values and principles that aim to define the organization's identity. Used by Johnson & Johnson and Champion International, such a code invites employees to make decisions based on the stated values.

To be effective, a code of values requires that employees understand the values, and therefore necessitates adequate training to help them apply the values to real-life cases. This type of code works only if there is a commitment to the stated values shared by everyone throughout the organization, a culture with a strong emphasis on autonomy, and an extensive organizational support system for the decision makers.

Code of Practice—an interpretation of the corporate values and principles *for* the employees along with a list of expected behaviors to convey clearly, "This is how we do things here." Also included, of course, is a statement of values and some explanation of how the expected behaviors have been derived from the corporate values. NYNEX's *Code of Business Conduct* falls into this category. While still addressing the employee as the ultimate decision maker, this type of code offers additional guidance and clarifies everyone's responsibilities.

Compliance Code—typically a list of rules, including prohibitions as well as affirmative duties. We see very few corporate ethics pamphlets that are exclusively of this type, though most contain at least one section that follows this format, usually the section(s) devoted to legal and regulatory requirements.

The best corporate ethics codes are a combination of all three formats:

Most essential is a **Code of Values,** which is the corporation's statement of its values and ethical principles. This provides the rationale for all that follows. If it is omitted (or if it is assumed that the values are implied in the text), the document rests on sand. The best codes contain a clear, unequivocal statement of the values and ethical principles of the corporation. In the **Code of Practice** section of the publication, the company's ethical principles must then be related to specific ethical issues and to common scenarios. Without it, employees may be at a loss as to how to apply the stated values. Finally, the publication should include a **Compliance Code** section dealing with applicable state and federal regulations that may be incorporated in the code.

Our Fab Five

After examining hundreds of codes with a combined format, these are our selections for the best examples:

GENERAL ELECTRIC'S
Integrity — Guide to Our Policies

NORTHROP GRUMMAN'S
Standards of Business Conduct

NYNEX's
Values and Ethics in Our Workplace

SEARS'
*Shared Beliefs/Leadership Principles/
Code of Business Conduct*

TELEDYNE'S
Ethics — Code of Business Conduct

You Can Leave Out the Kitchen Sink...

An effective ethics code should consist of more than just a list of rules and regulations. Let's take an element-by-element look at what the best ones contain:

I. General Letter to the Readers

It is common, though not universal, to find the first page of the organization's ethics code reserved for a letter from the chairman, president, or CEO. It is important to include such a letter, because it indicates that what follows is supported by the leadership of the organization. Of course actual ethical leadership and a willingness to "live the code" matters much more than a letter, but the letter has important symbolic value. A well-crafted letter is a good first step and its absence would be noted.

Though mostly of symbolic importance, the opening letter can also add value and substance to the code. For example, the letter can serve to highlight one or more aspects of the code and/or the ethics initiative itself. The letter accompanying the code of Pitney Bowes (see text opposite) does this.

The letter also can set the tone for what follows. It is important that it speak directly to each employee, but not in a preachy manner. Instead, references can be made to the importance of personal commitment and integrity, as expressed by Jack Welch in his letter to General Electric employees (see page 84). The author needs to convey to the reader the idea that commitment to ethical conduct is a shared responsibility, one that falls as much—or more—on executives as on others.

Letter from the
Chairman and President

Pitney Bowes was founded on the belief that the right of any business organization to exist is based upon the value of its products and services to its customers, and the benefits derived from its operations by others with whom it interacts, including stockholders, employees, suppliers, and the communities, states and nations where it does business.

That belief remains unchanged today, and is at the foundation of the Pitney Bowes' Value Statement, printed on the facing page. The simple, 13-point declaration describes our responsibilities to each of our constituents. However, it also forms the basis for the business conduct of the corporation and the employees in all its staff units and operating companies.

This Business Practice Guidelines booklet provides general conduct guidelines which complement the concepts expressed in the Values Statement. Every employee is expected to abide by them.

Many of these guidelines are based on law, while others are based on company policy. There are many sound business reasons for following their spirit as well as the letter of the laws under which we operate.

However, it is our belief that treating others with whom we do business, including our fellow employees, as we would want them to treat us—fairly, with courtesy and respect, and with the highest ethical and moral

standards—is the only course because it is the only course that is right.

For each of you, this booklet is your personal performance guide. When the responsibilities of your employment at Pitney Bowes present you with an opportunity, or confront you with a dilemma, let this book be your immediate reference. Various corporate and operating company procedure guides review in greater detail the prescribed conduct applicable to situations dealt with in the accompanying guidelines. These should be consulted as appropriate, and followed.

Be aware also, that the office of Corporate Ombudsman was established for you. Use the services of that office whenever you perceive any conflict between your job and these values.

I am confident that our employees understand and fully concur and comply with the company's commitment to conduct business courteously, fairly, legally, ethically, and morally. The publication of these guidelines is meant to ensure that Pitney Bowes will continue to be a company whose most precious value is the high standards it uses in balancing the needs and expectations of all of its constituents.

George B. Harvey
Chairman and President

Pitney Bowes: Ethics Code Cover Letter From the Chairman and President

Pitney Bowes was founded on the belief that the right of any business organization to exist is based upon the value of its products and services to its customers, and the benefits derived from its operations by others with whom it interacts, including stockholders, employees, suppliers, and the communities, states and nations where it does business.

That belief remains unchanged today, and is at the foundation of the Pitney Bowes' Value Statement.... The simple, 13-point declaration describes our responsibilities to each of our constituents. However, it also forms the basis for the business conduct of the corporation and the employees in all its staff units and operating companies.

This Business Practice Guidelines booklet provides general conduct guidelines which complement the concepts expressed in the Values Statement. Every employee is expected to abide by them.

Many of these guidelines are based on law, while others are based on company policy. There are many sound business reasons for following the spirit as well as the letter of the laws under which we operate.

However, it is our belief that treating others with whom we do business, including our fellow employees, as we would want them to treat us—fairly, with courtesy and respect, and with the highest ethical and moral standards—is the only course because it is the only course that is right.

For each of you, this booklet is your personal performance guide. When the responsibilities of your employment at Pitney Bowes present you with an opportunity, or confront you with a dilemma, let this booklet be your immediate reference. Various corporate and operating company procedure guides review in greater detail the prescribed conduct applicable to situations dealt with in the accompanying guidelines. These should be consulted as appropriate, and followed.

Be aware also, that the office of Corporate Ombudsman was established for you. Use the services of that office whenever you perceive any conflict between your job and these values.

I am confident that our employees understand and fully concur and comply with the company's commitment to conduct business courteously, fairly, legally, ethically, and morally. The publication of these guidelines is meant to ensure that Pitney Bowes will continue to be a company whose most precious value is the high standards it uses in balancing the needs and expectations of all of its constituents.

George B. Harvey
Chairman and President

**General Electric:
Statement of Integrity
From Chairman of the
Board and CEO**

For more than a century,
GE people have created
an asset of incalculable
value—the company's
worldwide reputation for
integrity and high stan-
dards of business con-
duct. That reputation,
built by so many people
over so many years,
rides on each business transaction we make.

Integrity is the rock upon which we build our business success—our quality
products and services, our forthright relations with customers and suppliers
and, ultimately, our winning competitive record. GE's quest for competitive
excellence begins and ends with our commitment to ethical conduct.

For each person in the GE community, I ask you to make a personal commitment to follow our Code of Conduct;

- Obey the applicable laws and regulations governing our business conduct
  worldwide.
- Be honest, fair and trustworthy in all of your GE activities and relationships.
- Avoid all conflicts of interest between work and personal affairs.
- Foster an atmosphere in which equal opportunity extends to every member
  of the diverse GE community.
- Strive to create a safe workplace and to protect the environment.
- Through leadership at all levels, sustain a culture where ethical conduct is
  recognized, valued and exemplified by all employees.

Guiding us in upholding our ethical commitment is a set of GE policies on key
integrity issues. All GE employees must comply not only with the letter of these
policies but also their spirit.

If you have a concern about what is proper conduct for you or anyone else,
promptly raise that concern to your manger of through one of the other channels the company makes available to you. Nothing—not customer service, competitiveness, direct orders from a superior or "making the numbers"—is more
important than integrity.

GE leaders have the additional responsibility to make compliance a vital part of
our business activities. Adherence to GE policy and applicable law is the foundation of our competitiveness. Concerns about appropriate conduct must be
promptly addressed with care and respect.

We are all privileged to work for one of the best companies in the world. We
must, every day in every way, preserve and strengthen for those who will follow us what has been GE's foundation for success for more than 100 years—
the GE commitment to total, unyielding integrity.

John F. Welch, Jr.
Chairman of the Board & Chief Executive Officer

The letter should not be threatening; instead it can, when appropriate, draw on a shared sense of commitment and tradition of service that everyone can be proud of. This is the approach taken by Colgate-Palmolive.

Colgate-Palmolive: Shared Commitment Letter From the Chairman and Chief Executive Officer

The reputation that the Colgate-Palmolive Company has built over the years for high ethical standards is one of our greatest business assets. Together, we share the responsibility to preserve and enhance this asset. Our goal has never been solely to comply with the law but to abide by the highest principles of integrity, honor and concern for others. As a company, we are committed to serving the best interest of all our varied constituencies: to increasing shareholder value, to providing consumers with safe, quality products, to offering opportunities for personal fulfillment to all Colgate people and to meeting our public responsibilities as a member of the global community.

The purpose of our Code of Conduct is to help you continue this tradition. It was first issued in 1987 and it is being reissued now in response to changes in our legal and business environment. The Code offers nothing new in basic content—every principle set forth here is part of our long-standing policy and practice. It is intended to reinforce and enhance our corporate culture, not to change it, and is distributed to each of you as a reminder of your Company's tradition of high ethical standards. The Code addresses issues of law, ethics, fairness and humanity that arise in the context of the following relationships: with fellow employees, with the Company, with outside business entities, with consumers, with governments, with society and finally, with shareholders.

It is impossible to describe how these principles apply to all the different situations facing each of us. In addition, we will inevitably encounter local laws, customers and practices which vary widely from place to place. Therefore, you have the responsibility to bring any questions you may have about these principles to the attention of your management.

We hope that the Code of Conduct contributes to our ongoing dialogue about the values and beliefs that make Colgate-Palmolive unique.

Reuben Mark
Chairman and Chief Executive Officer

Finally, the letter should be direct, forthright and sincere. If there have been problems in the recent past, for example, and if these are part of the reason why the code has been written or updated, this needs to be stated. A good representation of this type of candor is Hughes' pamphlet: "Integrity: Three Hughes Case Histories—What Went Wrong, Why It Went Wrong, and Lessons Learned." It is followed on pages 87 and 88 by the text of the first case history.

Hughes: "Integrity" Letter from C. Michael Armstrong, Chairman and CEO

Our Company has a strong, respected Code of Conduct and administrative processes in place to help us all adhere to standards of ethical business conduct. The leadership to ensure that we meet these standards must come from you and me, the management of our Company.

When we do not fulfill this responsibility, the results are damage to our reputation, diversion of resources for corrective action, and lowered employee morale— costs that we cannot afford.

Thus, management throughout the Company is expected to:
• Provide leadership and serve as role models;
• Be involved;
• Ensure everyone is trained in their ethics responsibilities and understands what is expected of them; and
• Seek immediate higher-level management counsel on any situation.

As a business of people committed to a high standard of conduct, we cannot accept anything less from each and every one of us.

The three case histories presented in this booklet are lessons from which we all can learn. They highlight what can go wrong when management fails in its responsibilities.

I hope we have no more examples to share with you in the future.

Hughes: "Integrity" Pamphlet Case History One

SCENARIO ONE

In preparation for an anticipated Government audit, Division X's general manager directed his Quality Assurance (QA) department to conduct an audit of manufacturing and testing records. In addition, he asked each manufacturing and test operation to gather one year's records for the Government audit team to review.

The internal audit team concluded that all the records were in order. However, one auditor mentioned to a supervisor that, although all data had been recorded correctly, the records maintained in her department were messy and in the future she should see to it that the operators working for her took greater care in making entries in those records.

The supervisor was embarrassed by the auditor's comments and afraid that a Government auditor might issue a negative finding about the neatness of her department's records. In an effort to avoid such a negative finding, the supervisor enlisted the help of one of her operators. Together, they:
• Recreated all of the year's records by copying the information from the original records onto new record sheets and inserting the newly created material into the original files;
• Corrected what they viewed as discrepancies in the records;
• Forged the initials of operators who had originally signed the paperwork, going so far as using different colored pens to reflect the colored pens used by each operator; and
• Discarded the original records.
When they were interviewed subsequently, both the supervisor and operator indicated that they were not aware that any of those activities were inappropriate.

Finally, another supervisor became suspicious when he saw the two employees throwing a lot of paper into a wastebasket. He retrieved the paper from the wastebasket and, believing the documents to be original manufacturing

In preparation for an anticipated Government audit, Division X's general manager directed his Quality Assurance (QA) department to conduct an audit of manufacturing and testing records. In addition, he asked each manufacturing and test operation to gather one year's records for the Government audit team to review.

The internal audit team concluded that all the records were in order. However, one auditor mentioned to a supervisor that, although all data had been recorded correctly, the records maintained in her department were messy and in the future she should see to it that the operators working for her took greater care in making entries in those records.

The supervisor was embarrassed by the auditor's comments and afraid that a Government auditor might issue a negative finding about the neatness of her department's records. In an effort to avoid such a negative finding, the supervisor enlisted the help of one of her operators. Together, they:

• Recreated all of the year's records by copying the information from the original records onto new record sheets and inserting the newly created material into the original files;
• Corrected what they viewed as discrepancies in the records;
• Forged the initials of operators who had originally signed the paperwork, going so far as using different colored pens to reflect the colored pens used by each operator; and
• Discarded the original records.

When they were interviewed subsequently, both the supervisor and operator indicated that they were not aware that any of those activities were inappropriate.

Finally, another supervisor became suspicious when he saw the two employees throwing a lot of paper into a wastebasket. He retrieved the paper from the wastebasket and, believing the documents to be original manufacturing records, sent them to QA. QA concluded that the records were originals and that some original records were missing. The QA manager immediately notified Division X's assistant general manager and advised him to call Sector Legal counsel. The assistant general manager told the QA manager that he would not do so but would, instead, conduct his own investigation. The assistant general manager did inform the Division's general manager and manager of Human Resources. The Division then conducted an investigation on its own.

The Government also conducted several lengthy, thorough investigations that highlighted practices that were wrong and embarrassing. While Hughes was not prosecuted, the Company did receive warnings against further misconduct.

Division management disciplined all involved employees. The two employees who disposed of documents were suspended and demoted. The QA manager received a written reprimand. The Division's general manager was reprimanded, and the Division's assistant general manager was transferred. The Human Resources manager also was given a written reprimand.

(continues)

Hughes "Integrity" Pamphlet Case History One, *continued*

Company Policies That Were Not Followed

- No Company property should have been destroyed or altered without permission.
- Management needed to demonstrate sound ethics by example.
- Management should have recognized the potential ethics violations when the information was reported.
- Management did not advise the Ethics Program Office of the potential ethics violations.
- Management had the responsibility to ensure that the problem was investigated thoroughly and corrected.
- Management was responsible for ensuring that underlying processes or procedures were reviewed and improved to eliminate the root causes that gave rise to the ethics issues.

Lessons Learned

1. Employees need to be trained on appropriate record keeping.
2. No one should ever revise or modify existing records. When writing is illegible, an explanation should be prepared on a separate sheet and attached to the original documentation.
3. All employees must advise the Ethics Program Office when they suspect a potential violation.

As an alternative to the opening letter, some corporations have instead interspersed highlighted quotations from corporate leadership throughout the publication, as does Texas Instruments. This accomplishes everything the opening letter does, but with at least two additional advantages: short blocks of copy are more likely to be read than a letter; secondly, quotations can be selected and placed within a publication in such a way as to highlight specific points being addressed in that section.

II. Mission and Strategy Statements

Following the introductory letter, statements on mission and strategy usually appear at the beginning of ethics codes. Johnson & Johnson, for example, starts with its Credo (opposite page), while Pitney Bowes uses a "values statement." Other organizations offer an untitled introductory paragraph to serve as a mission statement, an approach taken by New York Life. Citicorp presents an introductory section to the code that cites the mission statement and then explains how it relates to ethics.

Our Credo

Johnson & Johnson: Credo

We believe our first responsibility is to the doctors, nurses and patients, to mothers and all others who use our products and services. In meeting their needs everything we do must be of high quality. We must constantly strive to reduce our costs in order to maintain reasonable prices. Customers' orders must be serviced promptly and accurately. Our suppliers and distributors must have an opportunity to make a fair profit.

We are responsible to our employees, the men and women who work with us throughout the world. Everyone must be considered as an individual. We must respect their dignity and recognize their merit. They must have a sense of security in their jobs. Compensation must be fair and adequate, and working conditions clean, orderly and safe. Employees must feel free to make suggestions and complaints. There must be equal opportunity for employment, development and advancement for those qualified. We must provide competent management, and their actions must be just and ethical.

We are responsible to the communities in which we live and work and to the world community as well. We must be good citizens—support good works and charities and bear our fair share of taxes. We must encourage civic improvements and better health and education. We must maintain in good order the property we are privileged to use, protecting the environment and natural resources.

Our final responsibility is to our stockholders. Business must make a sound profit. We must experiment with new ideas. Research must be carried on, innovative programs developed and mistakes paid for. New equipment must be purchased, new facilities provided and new products launched. Reserves must be created to provide for adverse times. When we operate according to these principles, the stockholders should realize a fair return.

The key is that the mission and strategy statements, if included in any form, must be clearly linked to ethics. Probably the most serious error that could be made in this respect is to present a mission and strategy statement that makes no clear reference to ethics. Despite the fact that the mission statement may talk around ethics — by references to the organization's commitment to respecting employees as individuals, or its emphasis on teamwork and quality — "ethics" itself may be missing. Unfortunately it often does not appear until the last sentence, if at all. Though such an omission greatly reduces the impact of the mission statement, it can easily be remedied.

Under consideration is the following new and improved version of one company's mission statement referring explicitly to "ethics":

"As a leading healthcare company, our products and services play a direct role in helping people in need and improving the quality of life for all our customers. Therefore, we recognize that ethics is an integral part of who we are and what we do. Concern and respect for individuals, and commitment to the well-being of others; these are, and must be, our guiding values."

Errors of omission weaken strategy statements as well. To include a strategy section in an ethics pamphlet that does not mention ethics is, to say the least, highly problematic. Here too, however, the problem can be easily corrected. There is often an ethical dimension to much of what is expressed in strategy statements; it only needs to be brought out. A health care company, for example, can state unequivocally that "delivering effective therapy to patients in low-cost settings is not only profitable but is also the ethical and socially responsible thing to do."

III. Overview and Statement of Purpose

In most cases the opening letter and/or introductory section of the code includes an overview of the entire publication and a statement of its purpose. Employees often come up with questions and may be suspicious about the organization's underlying motives in publishing a code. These should be addressed directly. It is usually not enough to make a passing reference to social responsibility, or to regulatory requirements, or to upholding the company's traditions. More is needed, especially if employees doubt the motives and/or commitment of the organization's leadership. Carefully tailored focus groups can help elicit this undercurrent of feelings before the ethics code is finalized.

In developing ethics codes companies too often miss the opportunity to allay doubts and to begin the process of building trust. This can be accomplished either by incorporating a question and answer section or by adding a separate section explaining why the publication is being issued at all.

IV. Explanation of How to Use the Code

A critical component of any code is a clear statement of the company's expectations, how the code relates to other ethics initiatives, and what readers should do if they have questions or learn of possible wrongdoing. To meet these objectives, every publication should offer guidance as to the use of the code.

Some codes, such as General Electric's, are so comprehensive and complex that directions on their use are required. A better bet is to design the code in such a way that it is "user friendly" with a table of contents, index, quick reference guides, and other specific aids to its use. If written well, these are usually enough to help the reader navigate the publication.

In some cases there is no need for an explanation of how to use the code. A compact code of ethics, like Dow Corning's, can be scanned quickly. The compact version, unfortunately, cannot be complete and must be supplemented from time to time with additional materials to ensure that sufficient information is available.

V. Questions & Answers

A question and answer section in a code always gets high marks from readers. In fact, some codes are presented almost entirely in this format. One code that comes to mind is organized by business policy issues, replete with sections on financial record keeping and customer gifts. The questions posed and answered are cited as "common employee questions." If employees actually do have these questions, then they should find the format quite helpful. Examples from the Sears "Code of Business Conduct" are reprinted opposite.

If some of the more common employee questions are not to be found, then the format is highly problematic because it offers little guidance beyond the "question and answer." Employees may have interpersonal relations questions about favoritism, harassment, or discrimination. Not only would they be disappointed to find these missing, but they could also conclude that the company does not consider these issues to have any ethical import. It is possible, of course, to meet this objection while retaining the "question and answer" format by simply expanding the publication to cover other areas of concern.

SEARS

Code of Business Conduct

The business reputation of Sears rests with each associate

———

Sears: "Code of Business Conduct" Questions and Answers Samples

Q: While ringing up a sale recently, I noticed that an item was mismarked and the customer was being overcharged. The customer did not seem to notice, and there were many people waiting in line. Would it be all right not to mention the error?

A: No, it is never acceptable to over-charge a customer. Charge the customer the correct price and advise your manager that the item is mismarked.

Q: I am a sales manager. In conducting a routine package check, I find that merchandise sold by one associate to a fellow associate has not been charged or charged incorrectly. What should I do?

A: Both associates are responsible for the accuracy of this transaction. Contact Asset Protection personnel to interview both associates. Have the associate who made the purchase pay the amount due. Mistakes can happen, but such activity may indicate theft.

Q: I generally know the warranty for the products I sell. What is the policy if a customer asks to see the warranty? Do I always need to look up the exact terms?

A: Yes. If the customer asks to see the warranty, you are obligated under federal law to show the customer its text before they purchase.

Q: I think a competitor is misstating the performance on a product it offers. I don't want to lose the sale. Can I "talk up" or stretch the performance of the Sears product to clinch the sale?

A: No. The capabilities of the Sears product must always be accurately described. If you know the performance of the competitor's item, you should correct any misinformation the customer may have in a factual manner, without accusing the competitor of lying.

An alternative is to state briefly how these specific questions were chosen to the exclusion of others. Perhaps the company has conducted an employee survey, a needs assessment, or a focus group process, or perhaps it keeps records of questions that are frequently asked of managers, human resource personnel, security, or whomever. If so, then this should be explained in the publication. This will minimize the detrimental effect on those who might otherwise ask: "Why these questions? They're not my questions."

More importantly, if the "question and answer" format is used exclusively, there is always the potential problem that the questions and answers format cannot easily convey all the information that the code must convey, nor that it can easily cover all the topics that must be covered. For this reason it is better to include questions and answers while also relying on other means to deliver the intended message. This is the approach used by Northrop Grumman, Teledyne, and General Electric.

VI. Use of Mini Case Studies

Few ethics codes present mini case studies. Most organizations, NYNEX and Sears among them, incorporate case studies in their other ethics publications to supplement their codes. Still others work case studies into their ethics training. Using case studies in training or in other publications is a generally good approach. If the principal vehicle for conveying corporate values, ethics policies and procedures is the code, however, then it is critical to plant the studies firmly within the code itself.

VII. Summary of Resources/Where to Find Help

Corporate ethics codes should be able to refer the reader to other resources within and—if appropriate—outside the organization. These resources may include:

- Other corporate publications that discuss specific policies in more detail
- Personnel who can help clarify policy and to whom the employee can report possible wrongdoing

Most corporate codes attempt to offer guidance about the ethics officer or other personnel responsible for answering questions and helping employees. In many cases, however, the "guidance" is incomplete and/or confusing. In some codes, one section informs employees that it is their responsibility to report possible violations to their supervisor and/or the corporate law department, while another directs them to contact the corporate senior vice president of human resources, corporate general counsel, or the chairman of the public policy committee of the board. True, written codes should stress that reporting violations is an employee responsibility, but this approach opens the door for several problems and a number of missed opportunities.

- First, many corporations maintain a dedicated ethics telephone line, usually an 800 number, that can be called whenever the employee has a question about an ethics policy or believes she/he has information about an ethics violation. This number should be displayed prominently in the ethics pamphlet and in all corporate ethics publications, as is the Sears 1-800-ASSIST number (see page 96). Some codes name the contact office but do not include the phone number and/or address. This omission undoubtedly reduces the number of effective calls.

- Second, multiple avenues for reporting violations, especially if all are senior managers, may actually decrease the number of effective calls. Due to the complexities of ethics cases, the question of which person to call is frequently not easy to answer, and the caller is required to make what is likely to be an uncomfortable judgment. In addition, the caller must con-

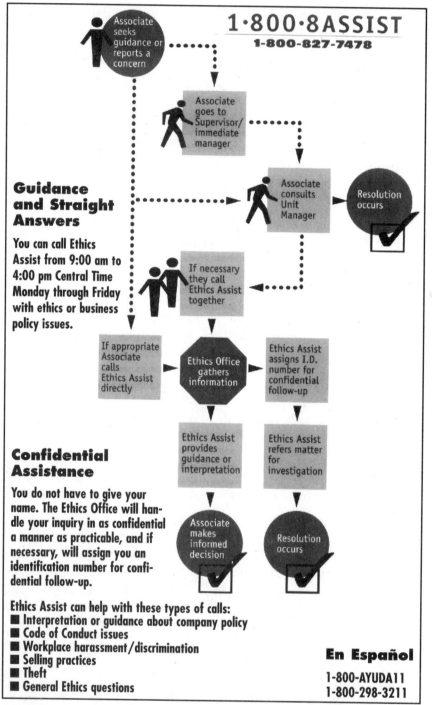

1·800·8ASSIST
1-800-827-7478

Guidance and Straight Answers

You can call Ethics Assist from 9:00 am to 4:00 pm Central Time Monday through Friday with ethics or business policy issues.

Confidential Assistance

You do not have to give your name. The Ethics Office will handle your inquiry in as confidential a manner as practicable, and if necessary, will assign you an identification number for confidential follow-up.

Ethics Assist can help with these types of calls:
- Interpretation or guidance about company policy
- Code of Conduct issues
- Workplace harassment/discrimination
- Selling practices
- Theft
- General Ethics questions

En Español

1-800-AYUDA11
1-800-298-3211

Sears: "Code of Business Conduct" 1-800-ASSIST Information

tact a senior manager, a daunting prospect for most employees in the best of circumstances. While multiple avenues for
calling may be given as an option in specific cases, corporations with effective ethics programs usually steer calls to the
ethics officer. This helps to address both of the above concerns.

- Third, too often codes suggest that employees call only if
they think they have witnessed a violation. General Electric,
Levi Strauss, McDonald Douglas, Northrop, NYNEX, and
countless other corporations take a different approach and
advertise the call line as a resource line, or a guidance or help
line. This minimizes the characterization that it is only a
"snitch line."

VIII. Finding Out What to Expect When Using the "Guideline"

The code should supply employees with basic information they
need in order to feel more at ease with the "guideline" process. By
the time an employee makes a call for assistance, the problem
being reported has usually existed for some time. Anxieties are
running high and mistrust and fear of the process complicate matters further. Some possible considerations for addressing this
problem in the code itself include the following:

- Are there other indirect ways employees can make an inquiry
or report a violation? Can they reach someone after-hours?
This is especially important if the employees are in small
work areas or if the ethical problem involves coworkers. To
solve this problem, Raytheon, for example, has an off-site
post office box. Texas Instruments has a secure, anonymous
e-mail system that is a direct line to the ethics officer.

- What sort of questions will employees be asked if they call? Most importantly, can they remain anonymous? The more mystery the code removes from the calling process, the better. One way to accomplish this is to describe a "typical" call in order to give the potential caller a better sense of what to expect and prepare for.

- What will happen after the call? Lockheed Martin, among others, has tried to address this question in its employee ethics training. Employees need to know if they can follow up to see what is being done. If there will be an investigation, they are entitled to be advised of this fact. They should be told who will be informed of the call. Will their supervisor be told, or will he or she otherwise be able to learn about it? Also, employees will want all the particulars of what steps will be taken to ensure that they need not fear retribution. If this cannot be guaranteed, assurances should be given that the company understands that there are risks involved and is taking specific steps to try and minimize them.

IX. Other Common Topics

Most corporate ethics codes include sections that address:

- Conflicts of interest
- Compliance with applicable laws
- Political contributions
- Payments to government officials
- Proprietary information and insider trading
- Gifts and entertainment
- Financial record keeping

We suggest the following topics should also be considered for inclusion:

- The environment and the employees' responsibilities
- Product safety
- Workplace safety
- Quality
- Diversity
- Employee health screening
- Privacy in the workplace
- The right to privacy outside of the workplace
- AIDS/HIV
- Work and family
- Sexual harassment
- Corporate due process
- Plant closures and downsizing
- Community service
- Disinvestment and international boycotts
- Executive compensation
- Affirmative action
- Employment at will

Far too often, sexual harassment and other issues involving interpersonal workplace relations are considered human resource problems and on that basis are excluded from the ethics manual and the ethics process. This is a mistake. From an ethicist's point of view, these acts can harm others and, consequently, are clearly ethical matters. They also involve issues of duty, rights, and responsibilities. From the employees' point of view, interpersonal workplace relations are often the most critical ethical problems they face. How these matters are handled says a great deal to employees about the organization's commitment to basic ethical principles of equity, fairness and respect.

The Author, Please!

Writing an ethics code may seem daunting, but doing so is well worth the time and effort. While business ethics consultants with extensive experience in developing codes and related material can facilitate the process, they should not write the actual code. An ethics task force or committee of company officers can tackle the project, but it is also important to draw upon as many employees as possible in the process. They can participate through surveys, focus groups, and task forces.

The important thing to remember is that the code should be their code. It should not be handed down from on high.

8

FROM THE GRASS ROOTS
"TELL IT LIKE IT IS"

We now know that an ethical climate must be set at the top, but it won't be effective unless all employees believe it is "for real." When asked, they speak frankly about their perceptions of effective ethical programs.

Recently, a corporation engaged us in a review of its ethics training program that was centered around revised ethics policies and its code of conduct. A focus group participated in the corporate ethics training session and participants were then questioned individually.

"Why do you think X is writing these policies and developing this training program?" was the question asked of each participant. Through the focus group we hoped to discover what preconceptions about the company, its ethics efforts, or corporate ethics in general the participants were bringing to the process. If they came into the process highly cynical, this situation would have to be addressed.

Some typical responses:

- "I assume they're doing this because they've had problems."
- "They're doing it as a matter of survival. It has to be done. We all know that."

- "These days it's standard policy to have guidelines. You have to spell out what everyone's responsibilities are."

- "They never discussed that, so people form their own opinions. I guess they've been hurt in the past. With all the regulations and attention to ethics these days ... it's reality. They have no control over all that, but they do have to cover themselves."

- "They'd be running a serious risk if they didn't lay out the policy. There are all kinds of consequences to these sorts of things."

In short, though the words differ, each participant was firmly convinced that the company was motivated by necessity, by the demands of the regulatory environment, and/or in response to the public's increased scrutiny of corporate behavior.

"Suppose this is their sole motivation. Do you think any less of their effort?" was our next question for the employees.

- Every participant answered that he or she did not.

"What was the *stated* reason for the policies and training program?" This question drew a sharp contrast between these sentiments and the participants' responses:

- Many commented that they couldn't really recall whether any specific rationale for the policies and program were given.

While discussing existing policies, participants did remember and refer to the *written statement by the company's CEO,* which was included as the first page of the Code. This actually made little or no impression on them, however.

- Participants repeatedly said they didn't believe the company was being "up-front" about its true motivations.

- One participant commented that this lack of candor was "contrary to the spirit of ethics."

- Another stated that this increased his initial cynicism: "I don't understand why they weren't more up-front about their reasons for doing all this. I can understand that they wouldn't want to dredge up past problems, but they could certainly have introduced the material in a more honest way. I felt like it was a smoke screen, a bit too vague."

One participant in the project offered a practical alternative. Her wisdom is worth repeating for the benefit of all organizations seeking to establish the right tone of cooperation and openness in its ethics communications:

- **Emphasize in the introduction to the Code the external pressures** on the company and industry that necessitate this type of initiative, including regulations, potential lawsuits, and increasing public attention to business ethics.

- **Specify the types of consequences that can result** when ethics is ignored. Be specific. Spell out consequences for the company as well as for employees. This should include not only economic threats but also a frank discussion of the sense of isolation and frustration on the job that can result when ethical dilemmas are ignored or when employees believe they are unresolvable.

- **In addition to "the stick," also discuss "the carrot."** Cite specific benefits to the company, its constituents and employees that can result if ethics is given priority. Perhaps discuss ethics in conjunction with quality or diversity, or other on-going initiatives.

- **Emphasize the potential benefits of these policies and programs for employees.** She even suggested this wording: "We understand the pressures you can find yourself confronted with, and so we've developed these policies to assist and support you as you grapple with difficult issues."

The interviewee who made these suggestions argued that candor can eliminate much of the initial cynicism, and she thought it would also create a more cooperative atmosphere of "we're all in this together." It is important to be candid and to make every effort to give employees a sense of ownership, both of the finished publication and the process as well. The introductory section of the Code should include material that sets a cooperative tone. It is a subtle change, but it is one that can increase employees' acceptance of, and commitment, to an ethics code.

So You Think You
Need an Ethics Officer...

We now know that many companies and organizations are appointing executives to oversee ethics programs to ensure that they retain **the ethical edge.** To understand why, perhaps an analogy to the world of finance is in order. Every employee in an organization is responsible for adhering to budgets, accounting for expenses and subscribing to sound financial procedures, yet financial oversight rests with the chief financial officer. So, too, cutting-edge companies, whether by prescience and conscience or forced by scandal, are now studying the position of Ethics Officer and working it into their organization chart. While ethics is the responsibility of everyone in the organization, someone has to ensure that ethics remains a priority and is integrated throughout the organization.

"...A What?"

Who are these folks and where do they come from?

- Some companies select an outstanding individual from within the company to fill the position, announce the appointment and then design the ethics office, its function, reporting lines, and staffing needs around that person. This approach is often the best way to establish credibility quickly, according to some ethics officers, particularly if the person selected is an insider who is well known and highly regarded throughout the organization. This is not always possible, however, particularly if senior executives themselves have been implicated in wrongdoing or have played a part in creating an unethical corporate culture. If there is no insider who, on the basis of his or her character and reputation alone, can lend credibility to the office, then an alternative approach is required.

- Some companies name an outsider to the position. Going outside the company works particularly well if the person named immediately brings credibility to the office through an unflawed reputation and a clean character slate. This approach has the advantage of lending a degree of objectivity to the office; a new face may be just what is needed in a time of cynicism and low morale.

- Other companies begin by designing the ethics office itself and announcing its structure and function prior to, or at the same time as, the announcement of the person who will fill the position. In this case it is the establishment of the "ethics office function" and not the announcement of the person filling the position that fosters trust. Someone who is relatively unknown can then be named to fill the position. In order for this approach to work, the design of the ethics office function must emphasize those characteristics that employees associate with objectivity and effectiveness, especially the traits of independence and authority.

How Not to Do It

If the person selected as ethics officer does not meet the "character and reputation test" but instead is seen only as a figurehead and not the one who would be directly responsible for running the ethics office, then little is gained and much credibility may be lost by the announcement of the appointment. For example, if the chief financial officer of a company is highly respected and on that basis is named the ethics officer, but while retaining many other duties, it will be clear to everyone that the announcement was only for appearances' sake. It would be far better to make an additional appointment or perhaps include the chief financial officer on an ethics advisory or policy committee. Above all, the initial appointment must be seen as sincere and meaningful.

A Renaissance Person

The perfect ethics officer, according to such experts as Graydon Wood and Christopher Martin Bennett of NYNEX, is a complete blend of wisdom and skills. He or she

- is at a high level and a true officer of the company;
- operates with unrestricted access to the chief executive officer and the board of directors, or a committee of the board;
- maintains a high degree of trust and respect among members of the senior management team;
- can assemble resources for affecting internal procedural changes and carrying out investigations;
- has access to information and support mechanisms that provide monitoring, measuring, early warning and detection;

- offers incentives and rewards for proactively carrying out the compliance role; and

- has the skills to operate effectively with the press, public forums and the legal process.

NYNEX View of the
Role of the Corporate Ethics Officer

A Leader! Proactive vs. Reactive!

A Driver of Values and Standards

An Interpreter

A Communicator

An Educator

A Confidant and Counselor

A Pragmatist

A Visionary and Optimist

An Enforcer

An Image Maker

A Value Adder!

"An unswerving commitment to people,
trust in their basic goodness and confidence in the future."

How About Someone From Finance, Legal or HR?

Selecting an executive from the financial, legal, or human resources departments may appear to be an easy solution. Financial officers already have responsibilities and infrastructure support involving the integrity of accounting practices and other internal financial controls, and the chief financial officer already enjoys direct access to the CEO and the board of directors. With extensive experience in validating internal control and procedures, internal auditors are specialists in performing independent reviews. Legal officers bear responsibility for compliance with the law and no doubt have gained the credibility and skills to handle sensitive problem-solving, particularly when it involves allegations of civil or criminal wrongdoing. HR managers routinely work with employees on diversity, equal employment opportunity, harassment and other sensitive issues.

In all three cases, though, there may be conflicts between a financial, legal, or HR executive's primary loyalties and responsibilities and the functions an ethics officer must perform. On balance, the wiser course may be to call on such individuals to serve as resources for the ethics officer and the ethics compliance effort. The best ethics officers may be those who have a wide range of management experience within their organization.

An Impossible Job?

Even the most savvy and experienced ethics officers sometimes find themselves overwhelmed with the tasks at hand. We understand why. Organizations expect their ethics officers to

- meet with employees, the board, and top management, to discuss, advise and report on corporate ethics;
- create and disseminate the code of conduct and other ethics compliance publications and internal documents;
- create and maintain reporting systems such as hotlines, helplines, and guidelines;
- oversee investigations of alleged wrongdoing;
- review and modify the code of conduct as needed;
- monitor adherence to laws and to the code of conduct;

- provide ethics training at all levels of the organization;
- assess the effectiveness of ethics programs;
- deal with the press, investors, community groups, customers and others affected by the company's practices or conduct.

The Effective Ethics Officer — Less Is More

Ethics officers don't usually broadcast their activities. In many companies, the position of ethics officer is a new one and the functions are still being developed. Experienced ethics officers have learned to avoid the limelight, cautioning that publicity will result in a loss of their effectiveness and many lead to the airing of company problems that are better left confidential. Ethics officers are sensitive that their position and authority in an organization not look like a public relations ploy. This sensitivity to public exposure is often what helps make so many of them so valuable.

Guidance From Those in the Know

While the responsibilities of ethics officers may vary from company to company and industry to industry, ethics officers are in general agreement about what makes them effective. Here's what they suggest:

DON'T become identified with top management. If this happens, an ethics officer will appear to have lost objectivity, and it is less likely that problems will be brought to his or her attention by employees in all ranks of the organization. This means the lofty ethics officer will be cut off from the very channels of communication needed to find out what really is going on.

DO work to have access to everyone in the organization, from top to bottom—the board of directors, senior and middle management and all employees, in all states and countries. Stay central.

DON'T just give simplistic interpretations of the code of ethics in response to problems. If employees wanted a simple answer, they could figure one out for themselves.

DO make an effort to analyze the general values and principles stated in codes of ethics and then apply them to specific situations as they arise. An ethics officer's first duty is to help recognize potential ethical problems that might be obscured by operational or financial considerations and then to lend expertise to resolving the problems.

DON'T view the position of ethics officer as banishment to "corporate Siberia" or allow others to view it that way. Don't appear to be hiding out on "the gold coast" or top floor of corporate headquarters.

DO keep involved in day-to-day operations of the organization so as to stay close to fast-breaking issues such as sexual harassment, deceptive sales practices, drug testing, compliance with existing or proposed regulations, customer complaints and ongoing training, to name just a few. Maintain an open door policy and get to know others from all departments.

DON'T assume that wrongdoing will be resolved just because the ethics officer holds senior executive status or because he or she reports to the chief executive officer.

DO insist on direct reporting authority to the board of directors as well as to the chief executive officer. Some of the toughest problems occur when the ethical conduct of senior management is in question.

DON'T hand off responsibility for the oversight or conduct of investigations to someone else, especially not to a faceless committee.

DO stay actively involved in the investigation process to ensure accountability. Keep watch on the progress of investigations to maintain the integrity of the investigation and to facilitate the task of reporting back to the accuser. Open and close all cases personally. Even if an outside consulting firm is doing the actual investigation, only hands-on oversight promotes consistency and provides reassurance to employees that the ethics officer they trust, not a third party, is ultimately handling the investigation.

DON'T ignore the risks of conflicts of interest or appearances of favoritism in some investigations or on sensitive issues.

DO choose an outside investigator or consultant to handle cases in which the ethics officer or his or her function may be perceived as having a conflict; continue, however, to coordinate and oversee the investigative process.

DON'T try to do too much and thereby shortchange investigations or their resolution. Not all ethics officers have the time and resources to conduct every investigation personally, and not all ethics officers are trained in investigative methods.

DO remember that the integrity of the process and the results of the investigation are of primary concern. Use outside help when needed, particularly if the outside expertise will lend additional credibility and objectivity to the issue at hand. In the end, the effectiveness of the ethics officer and ethics compliance will increase.

DON'T assume that every investigation must be conducted with the same standards as a legal trial, making the process seem too formal and legalistic to employees. The result may be to discourage communication and to position the ethics officer as an obstacle to problem solving, rather than a resource. In many cases, a pragmatic answer is what is needed.

DO establish a process that allows for prompt and practical resolutions to problems while treating all employees with respect. Employment is not the same as citizenship. Those accused of wrongdoing do not have to be warned that they are being investigated or questioned. In most organizations, employment is a privilege. As long as employees are treated fairly, resolutions of ethical violations can be carried out without overly legalizing the process.

DON'T get bogged down in turf battles. Human resource personnel, corporate counsel, security, line supervisors and others may all be involved in ethical investigations, but they also may have their own policies and standards that can interfere with an ethical resolution of an issue.

DO insist on a higher standard of conduct than individual departments may urge. Being ethical involves taking responsibility, exercising judgment and being true to the spirit as well as the letter of the law. Ethics officers must remind all departments of the meaning of ethics or its simple essence will get lost in the bureaucracy.

DON'T allow cynicism to undermine an ethics program. Cynics believe that ethics officers and senior management are all talk and have no real commitment to new ethics initiatives. They believe that in a crunch, ethics will be the first to go.

DO make sure that ethics policies are communicated throughout the organization in a way that commands attention and reduces cynicism. Be alert for feedback that indicates that the communication is not effective.

DON'T give the appearance of a double standard.

DO communicate a consistent policy and a consistent application of that policy, as well as timely resolutions. Policies and procedures must apply equally within the entire organization.

DON'T just pass down edicts from on high. Cynicism is fostered if employees sense that their input is not taken seriously.

DO make overt efforts to listen. Not only will employees listen best if they believe that the ethics officer is listening too, but listening also has the advantage of ensuring that the ethics message is getting through the corporate hierarchy. If employees complain that the only person they hear speak about ethics is the ethics officer, then the ethics officer knows that training and communication at the line manager level must be reassessed, and that ethics must continue to be integrated into day-to-day operations.

What Works

Ethics officers are often singular individuals in their companies or organizations, and it can be lonely at the top. But when they get together, ethics officers are generous about sharing ideas and stories of what works.

- First and foremost, the ethics officer and senior management must do more than just talk about ethics. The most effective way of defeating cynics and developing a strong ethical culture is for senior management to be seen acting in accordance with the stated corporate values. If the corporation says in its code of ethics that volunteerism and community service are encouraged, then the CEO should be a community volunteer.

The Ethical CEO — Face to Face

Robert Haas, the CEO of Levi Strauss, has demonstrated his company's commitment to social responsibility by personally helping to distribute AIDS information pamphlets from a table in the company atrium.

Another CEO underscores his company's commitment to open lines of communication and business ethics by meeting with every new domestic employee. New employees, often in small groups, meet with him for a discussion of corporate values followed by an exchange of questions and answers. Such actions go a long way toward defeating the cynics.

- Ethics officers recommend that a critical part of their job be development of effective communication vehicles to report their activities to employees. Often an ordinary ethics newsletter won't do; employees seldom read them. A better idea is to incorporate ethics reports into an existing, popular, internal publication. Many companies publish employees' actual questions or problems together with a brief response. Some, to show how the system works, publish actual cases.

- Many ethics officers underscore the value of the effort in creating a corporate culture that is positive and one in which everyone can take pride. These companies emphasize ethical success stories.

A Few Thoughts on Ethics

One retired ethics officer emphasizes: "There's a difference between creating bounty hunters and recognizing sustained behavior. We recognized the latter."

Texas Instruments often makes the point in its literature that ethics requires social responsibility and individual commitment to community organizations. Consequently, the company regularly features employee community volunteers in its advertising.

- Many ethics officers recommend incorporating ethics into the performance appraisal process, thereby committing managers to a course of action that includes ethical considerations. While "measuring" ethics may seem difficult to do, ethics officers have developed successful tools by building issues of values into performance review questions. Effective questions during the review process yield the added benefit of enhancing overall ethics communications in all parts of the organization while avoiding unnecessary jargon. Perhaps most importantly, ethics performance appraisals put ethics where it belongs: squarely in the midst of day-to-day business operations.

Many Heads Are Better Than One

What do companies like Fidelity, American Express, Bell Atlantic, Levi Strauss, Colgate-Palmolive, Raytheon, Sears, Textron, and Pitney Bowes have in common? They are all members of the national Ethics Officer Association (EOA), and as such act as role models for their corporate peers in supporting new initiatives in the field of business ethics.

The EOA was formed in 1991 as a national forum for the exchange of information and strategies on ethics, compliance and business conduct programs; it is dedicated to promoting ethical business practices within both profit and nonprofit organizations.

Based in Waltham, Mass., at the Center for Business Ethics at Bentley College, which facilitates its activities, the Association has grown from just 30 members to more than 250. It now includes ethics officers from all industries, as well as major nonprofits and government entities. Membership in the EOA is exclusively for those who hold management status within an organization, have the assigned responsibility for devising and/or administering ethics and compliance programs, and desire to increase knowledge in the field. Since its inception, the EOA has held conferences or workshops twice a year for participants to learn new techniques, meet experts in their field, confront emerging ethical issues, discuss the nature of their job and its responsibilities, and work toward the resolution of common concerns.

10

"YOU MEAN, I'M GOING TO JAIL?!"
ALL ABOUT THE U.S. SENTENCING GUIDELINES

We now know that almost everyone in the business community has heard something about the Federal Sentencing Guidelines for Organizations. The Guidelines, which went into effect November 1, 1991, require judges and prosecutors to take into consideration "aggravating and mitigating" factors when they determine the fines and the length of probation for organizations convicted in federal courts. This consideration can be of crucial importance to a company, especially when facing multimillion-dollar fines, consent decrees, corporate probation—all because of wrongdoing on the part of employees. The particulars of jail terms for executives were spelled out in an earlier set of Federal Guidelines.

The mitigating factor receiving the most attention from business ethicists is the one that states that if an organization had in place, prior to the offense, "an effective program to prevent and detect violation of law," this program can reduce its fine by up to 60 percent. In general, business ethicists are enthusiastic about this provision because it encourages businesses to take steps that

The Federal Sentencing Guidelines:
A Brief History

In 1984, the United States Congress passed a crime bill that created a new government body called the U.S. Sentencing Commission. This Commission was given the responsibility for making the sentencing of those convicted of federal crimes more uniform and, in some cases, more harsh.

By 1987, the Commission completed Guidelines for the sentencing of individuals in federal courts (kidnappers, money-launderers, drug dealers, and others). Several judges resigned from the bench in objection to the harshness of the sentences and to the fact that they were required to follow the Guidelines.

The Commission then turned to organizations that could be considered culpable for the wrongdoing of their employees. The result was the 1991 Federal Sentencing Guidelines for Organizations.

The 1991 Guidelines take a "carrot and stick" approach. The "stick" is the threat of fines of up to $290 million. The "carrot" is the opportunity to reduce possible fines by putting in place an "effective program to prevent and detect violations of law," that is, an ethics program.

enhance the moral culture of their organizations, including establishing ethics initiatives. As a result, many large organizations have already reviewed their policies and programs, conducted risk assessments, and taken steps to ensure that their organizations are in compliance with the Guidelines' provisions.

Unfortunately, some companies and institutions have ignored the Guidelines. *Many smaller businesses, partnerships, and non-profit organizations have mistakenly concluded that the Guidelines do not apply to them.* Still others, though aware of the scope of the Guidelines, are nevertheless taking a wait-and-see approach. For the time being, these organizations are effecting only minimal changes to try and meet the letter of the Guidelines

---

"Give Us a Break, Judge"

How to qualify for the "mitigating factors" provision? Under the Federal Sentencing Guidelines, an organization must do all of the following:

- Establish standards and procedures for employees and other agents that are reasonably capable of reducing the prospect of criminal conduct
- Assign specific individual(s) the responsibility to oversee compliance with standards and procedures
- Use due care in delegating oversight responsibility
- Create methods for communicating standards and procedures such as training programs and publications
- Implement methods for achieving compliance such as establishing monitoring and auditing systems and/or reporting systems designed to that employees and others can report wrongdoing without fear of retribution

Further, an organization must be able to document that there has been a history of consistent enforcement of standards, and it must have in place procedures for modifying the policies and programs after an offense has been detected.

without making significant commitments. They argue that before they commit to new policies and programs, it is prudent to wait until some other unlucky organization is actually sentenced under the Guidelines. Then, if needed, they'll make more appropriate, large-scale responses, based on that case. Is this latter approach wise, or is it short-sighted, risky, or possibly even foolhardy?

We think it is foolhardy.

Obviously, establishing an "effective program" can represent a considerable undertaking and can divert attention and resources from other necessary business endeavors. Given the initial cost and effort, and coupled with the fact that little publicity has been given to the 200 or so organizations already sentenced under the Guidelines, it's not surprising that many organizations are choosing to implement a bare minimum program in the hope that it will be enough for the time being.

Some companies, for example, rather than establish the new position of ethics/compliance officer, are instead claiming that this function has always been performed by the corporate counsel, or secretary, or director of human resources. While in some cases this may be true, it seems clear that a fully implemented "effective program" requires more than part-time oversight.

Or, rather than create an ethics/compliance training program that reaches all employees on a periodic basis while targeting employees with specific ethics/compliance exposures, some organizations merely assign their new hires the task of reading the company's ethics code. It's hard to imagine any case in which such a "training program" would be judged adequate and in compliance with the Guidelines.

Are such minimal compliance efforts a prudent risk? They're not, of course, if an organization is among those sentenced under the Guidelines. Only those policies and programs in place *prior to the offense* will automatically count toward mitigation. In some cases prosecutors and judges have considered post-offense changes when deciding how to proceed, but there are no guarantees. In general, there is no chance to reduce a fine by beefing up the program after the fact.

The minimalist approach carries additional risk. We should expect that prosecutors will initially be looking carefully at companies with sham or minimalist programs because these cases will provide the best opportunity for setting precedent and spelling out what is and is not in compliance with the Guidelines requirements.

Further, it's hard to see what is to be gained from postponing the inevitable. The "effective program" provision is not likely to go away or be significantly watered down. Experts on the Guidelines have noted that the "effective program" provision is very "portable" and is even now becoming the standard description of an ethics/compliance program. As such, it has already begun to turn up in other guidelines and regulations.

Finally, the best reason for fully implementing ethics/compliance programs is that they do improve corporate ethics—a worthy goal for its own sake.

SECTION THREE

ETHICAL SURPRISES
WHEN ENOUGH WAS NOT ENOUGH

11

DOW CORNING
FIRST, KILL ALL THE LAWYERS

It seems hard to believe that a company ranked in the top 250 in the country for annual sales and in the top 100 for profits would file for bankruptcy a few years later—thanks to a product that represented a mere one percent of its sales. This is the story of Dow Corning and its silicone breast implants, which thousands of women claimed ruptured and leaked into their bodies, causing debilitating medical conditions. For years students of business ethics will no doubt study, with lively debate, what really happened. But it is not too soon to raise questions.

Is Dow Corning a company with a well-deserved reputation for ethics and integrity (instituting a senior level Code of Conduct Committee in 1976 and a code of conduct in 1977)? Or is it, as some have alleged, one of the most unethical companies in recent history?

Did Dow Corning turn a deaf ear to scores of complaints from customers and their doctors about serious medical problems resulting from the use of its product, or were each and every one of the concerns addressed in an open, scientifically rigorous debate?

Did Dow Corning ignore the resignation of one of its engineers over lack of safety testing, as was reported, or did the engineer resign for reasons not related to the product safety issue and only later put this spin on his departure?

Did Dow Corning attempt to destroy a survey conducted by outside researchers that disclosed severe medical problems associated with its product, or was the survey itself discredited because it seriously overstated the danger?

Did Dow Corning respond to a jury verdict awarding one of its customers $1.5 million in punitive damages and $211,000 in product liability damages by asking the court to seal the records in the case, in an effort to avoid alerting other customers and to quash further investigation; or was it legitimately concerned that a release of proprietary information would be unethical and harm stockholders, employees, and others?

When faced with public allegations that the company had hidden negative test results and lied to the public about the safety of its products, did Dow Corning's board of directors stonewall, continue to manufacture and sell the product, and continue to fight customers who brought suit alleging injury; or is this not at all what happened in the board meetings?

The real story may be difficult to discern in the face of charges and countercharges. Dow Corning's tale could be a story of an ethics program that didn't work, or it could be a story of an ethical company that has been unfairly accused without all the facts being known.

A Culture of Ethical Complacency or Ethical Excellence?

Dow Corning seemed to have learned from the lessons of its parent, Dow Chemical, itself sullied by Vietnam War-era allegations that it manufactured napalm and other toxic products. Dow Corning worked hard to win a reputation as an ethical company and it earned employee loyalty. Company executives instituted several ethics initiatives and there was no reason to suspect that these programs wouldn't do their job.

When Dow Corning began to manufacture and market silicone breast implants, the company regarded its entry into the business as fully in keeping with its corporate commitment to health care products that improve patients' lives and in finding new uses for silicone. Despite sporadic questions from customers and their doctors regarding the product and mysterious illness and disabilities, Dow Corning remained committed to the hundreds of thousands of women who were losing breasts to cancer and desperately seeking effective replacements.

Furthermore, Dow Corning's own scientists disagreed about the conclusiveness of safety studies. Internal disagreements were not discouraged; in fact, it was recognized that these were essential for scientific research and development. To this day the company regards internal freedom to disagree as one of its ethical strengths. It's ironic that these disagreements and the high level of candor within the company would later cloud the company's ethical reputation.

Notwithstanding the reports of medical problems from some implant recipients, Dow Corning continued to sell the product, which was in great demand. No doubt, the decision about whether to continuing selling implants or to withdraw them from the market was an ethical toss-up. In the end, the manufacturer continued to offer silicone implants for sale after being assured by scientists that it was safe to use them.

Some critics have argued that the company had enough reason to consider the implants dangerous. Thomas Talcott, a materials engineer, quit his job in 1976 and later began a new career as an expert witness in implant trials. He and others say he left Dow Corning in a dispute over the safety of the implants. If true, such a resignation should have been cause for alarm and review. Dow Corning agrees with that premise but insists that this was simply not the case. When Talcott left, the company says it was disturbed by the possibility that he might have taken proprietary information to a competitor. The issue of the safety of implants was not its concern when dealing with his resignation. Nor, they say, did they think it was his either at the time.

Internal debate continued. In 1983, in response to a Food and Drug Administration (FDA) recommendation, one of Dow Corning's researchers suggested further study on the implants. Complaints from customers continued to come in, but it was not until one plaintiff, Maria Stern, had her attorney look into Dow Corning's files that the questions about the company's ethical decision making began to arise. The documents in the file appeared damaging to Dow Corning, leading business magazine headlines to proclaim years later, "What did the industry know, and when?"

Stern won her case and the judge reprimanded Dow Corning for hiding internal documents that might have alerted other women and warned the company to investigate silicone safety.

Enter the Lawyers

There is a very good reason why many companies do not allow its ethics function to report to company counsel. A good legal course of action may not be a good ethical decision. The pressures of responding to a public relations nightmare on one side and a cadre of fee-hungry plaintiff attorneys on the other can lead to disaster. There is no better demonstration of that principle than the Dow Corning story.

It's difficult not to listen to lawyers. They are skilled debaters and speak with authority. They often occupy a high place in the organization and can spin tales of horrors if executives fail to "heed sound legal advice." In fact, faced with a crisis, the usual executive response is to "bring in the lawyers on this." No one is allowed to make a move without "checking with legal," and it is the rare executive who has enough self-confidence and moral integrity to say, "I don't care what the lawyers say. This is the right thing to do."

Dow Corning's lawyers fought Maria Stern all the way, and in the end, their response to the Stern award of $1.5 million in 1984 was to ask the court to seal the records from the public so that no other plaintiff or customer could learn of the testimony given at the trial. Legally, this may have been a sound decision, protecting proprietary company information and allowing open and free dissent within company ranks. Scientifically, while internal and external debate continued, Dow Corning relied on studies and medical opinion concluding that the implants were safe. In hindsight, instead of giving the appearance that the documents were not public, the company could possibly have been able to avoid allegations of cover-up and betrayal by being straightforward with all the material that was available at the time. Critics argue that this would have been a better course of action, permitting future implant recipients access to whatever the company then knew about the product's safety.

The FDA began paying attention to the public outcry about silicone implants and subsequently asked Dow Corning to turn over the records of its tests and experiments. Dow Corning agreed, but with the usual legal caveat: they must not be publicly disclosed. Dow Corning was responding with what *Business Week* called a "full-court press" to keep its studies from reaching the public.

Dow Corning's lawyers must have been getting nervous, however. In November 1990, the company was criticized by a federal judge for keeping health and safety information private, and the judge ruled that a public citizens' group had a right to see what Dow Corning was submitting to the FDA. Dow Corning's lawyers appealed, but the cat was getting out of the bag.

A National Center for Health Statistics (NCHS) survey of surgical devices, including silicone implants, apparently contained damaging news. What happened next shows how difficult it is to make pronouncements about who is acting ethically and who isn't. One of Dow Corning's former executives—who was not a party to the incident—states that a company epidemiologist was asked to destroy all of her copies of the unfavorable survey on the theory that it would undercut Dow Corning's assertions that it believed its product was safe.

All of the parties involved at Dow Corning insist that no one was asked to destroy documents and no documents were destroyed; the epidemiologist in question has also sworn to this under oath. The actual story, the company asserts, is that the

NCHS survey was flawed. By dramatically undercounting the number of women who had implants, it arrived at a higher complication rate, and even the FDA later agreed the figures were incorrect.

Meanwhile, the legal business was booming on both sides. In 1988 Mariann Hopkins sued Dow Corning, alleging that her connective tissue and immune system diseases were caused by the rupture of her silicone implant. Dow Corning's legal response? That Hopkins' suit was filed too late and her case should be dismissed. The court disagreed, and in 1991 awarded Hopkins $7.3 million in damages for fraud and product safety violations.

After the Hopkins award, the public learned firsthand of Dow Corning's prior knowledge of the questions about the silicone implants. Additional plaintiffs emerged by the hundreds, no doubt spurred on by aggressive personal injury lawyers who saw deep pockets, sympathetic cases, and conflicting evidence.

Dow Corning's response to the Hopkins award was to call the verdict outrageous and to appeal — a perfectly logical legal strategy, since there was evidence Hopkins' medical problems predated the implants. Though a legal reasonable approach, the strategy did not help in the court of public opinion. The court of appeals upheld the verdict and the award. Dow Corning's legal response was to keep appealing.

Hopkins' case eventually went all the way to the U.S. Supreme Court, which let the jury award stand. At that point, Dow Corning was ready to just pay Hopkins and put this troublesome case behind it. But the bickering among her many lawyers over their share of the award was so fractious that the company finally gave the money to the judge to parcel out.

Lawyers always win in the end. The defense strategy — deny, stonewall, defend — was a full-employment act for Dow Corning attorneys. And plaintiff attorneys were on the march, assisted by a phalanx of doctors who received bulk referrals from lawyers and ran assembly line practices to help women collect awards. By the end of 1992, Dow Corning was faced with more than 5,000 lawsuits; by 1994, the total would reach 12,000.

The implant manufacturer threw in the towel in 1993 and suggested an international settlement in excess of $4 billion for all breast implant claims, with Dow Corning's share to be as much as $2 billion. By 1995, 440,000 women had registered for the settlement, but another 15,000 women opted out, preferring to try their luck at individual lawsuits similar to what Stern and Hopkins had done.

The Bottom Line

Dow Corning may be right in the end. Scientific studies continue to show there is no link between silicone implants and connective tissue disease. If there is a link, and many believe there is, it may never be proven in a way that meets rigorous scientific standards. In 1992, a federal advisory committee voted unanimously to allow further use of silicone implants. According to Dr. Elizabeth Connell, chairman of the panel, there was no "clear cause-and-effect relationship" established between the implants and connective tissue disease.

But scientific proof may be beside the point. Because Dow Corning became embroiled in a national controversy with ethical implications involving one of its products, the impact has already been felt on its bottom line. Today the company finds itself in the middle of an ethical debate.

In 1992, Dow Corning lost $72 million and Moody's downgraded its debt. Dow Corning lost $284 million in 1993 and by that time its profit ranking had fallen to 465th. Dow Corning still had plenty of sales; by 1994 its revenues were more than $2 billion, but it reported a $6.8 million loss.

Red ink was not the final story, though. The breast implant controversy had become the tail that wagged the dog, affecting the parent companies as well. Dow Corning had been formed 50 years earlier as a joint venture of the Dow Chemical Company and Corning, Inc. The two parents adopted a hands-off posture toward their multinational offspring, except to cash the annual dividend checks it generated. Now the child had hit upon hard times and was looking for relief. In 1995 Corning, Inc. was forced to include a charge of $365 million against its own results due to Dow Corning's losses, while Dow Chemical initially found itself liable for a portion of a $5.2 million award won by retired nurse Gladys Laas for her illnesses. Could a parent company sit on the sidelines and pretend it was not a player in the implant litigation? Did it matter that the litigation was against a distinct, separate company? Dow Chemical's legal involvement is still disputed.

Bring in New Lawyers

The litigation defense lawyers were becoming overwhelmed as the number of victims and aggressive attorneys continued to grow. Suddenly, a $4.25 billion settlement fund—the largest single liability settlement in history—was looking like small change in the

face of the claims against the fund, and the breast implant controversy was still threatening to engulf the two parent companies.
It was time for a new legal team to take the field.

Bankruptcy lawyers prepared their papers and Dow Corning
filed for bankruptcy on May 15, 1995, doing just what angry
plaintiffs had predicted the company might do a year earlier
despite its attorneys' protestations to the contrary. The company
was well aware that public reaction to the bankruptcy filing would
be negative, and discussion at the board meeting was intense.
Which was the more ethical course of action?

- To continue to spend money to defend the company, not
  knowing whether it would ever be successful but certain that
  it would be depleting research and other funds? Or,

- To stop the process, resolve the implant cases, give money to
  the claimants, save the company and allow it to operate, continuing to generate funds for future settlements?

The board chose bankruptcy, freezing all lawsuits against the
two parent companies, as well as freezing all debts and claims
against Dow Corning, but allowing the company to continue to
operate. The company's bankruptcy filing instantly made all the
women with breast implant claims creditors of the company, and
delayed the settlement of all the claims by years.

Two weeks later, a bankruptcy judge refused the company's
request to shield its two parents from liability, and, as predicted,
outrage over the bankruptcy filing was severe. Finally, in
September of 1995, in face of the overwhelming number of claims
filed, federal Judge Sam C. Pointer declared the initial global settlement dead. A newspaper editorial lamented the fact that "an

otherwise viable business, and the jobs that go with it, might go down the drain of tort practice."

Too Little, Too Late

Could the Dow Corning story have turned out differently? Perhaps only legal, business, medical, and ethics historians will know, after the full story has played out.

It's not often that a company gets a test of its ethics code and commitments on this level. By comparison, resolving time card disputes and conflicts of interest is child's play. It's not until something of the magnitude and complexity of the breast implant controversy that the public really gets to see how a company's ethical culture fares. Dow Corning insists its ethical foundation met the test.

Dow Corning's Code of Conduct Committee (CCC) was established in 1976, one of the earliest in major companies, and was the forum for auditing and reporting business practices and airing ethical issues. At many junctures in the development, manufacture, and marketing of the silicone implants, internal disagreements were discussed and decided by the CCC and by others throughout the company. These centered around the sufficiency of research, the response to customer complaints, proper disclosures made to customers, physicians and health authorities, the company's responsibility to women who needed implants and its response to public concern about the product

Did the CCC work? John E. Swanson, a retired Dow Corning executive and former secretary of the CCC, characterizes the company's decision making as "corporate betrayal" of the principles it asserted and says the members of the CCC knew very little about the company's health care businesses. Swanson's own wife, in fact, became one of the company's plaintiffs, after years of illness due to her implants.

Company executives who were involved in the CCC decision-making process said that the process did work; issues were aired with candor, no documents were destroyed and the chair of the CCC, Richard Hazelton, later rose to the position of chief executive officer of the company.

Did the board of directors do its job? By the June 1991 meeting of Dow Corning's board of directors, the public furor over silicone breast implants was running high. Some company executives thought it was time for the CCC and the company to review Dow Corning's principal position about remaining in the implant business, and recommended as such. But the board decided that it was more important to keep its commitment to women by continuing to supply the product, despite the fact that there were no profits in doing so. The board may also have been listening to the lawyers, possibly fearing that suspending sales would look like an admission of wrongdoing. Those involved in the decision said that to stop selling would have been an easier decision, but the board decided to stay in the implant business.

Did an outside investigation work? By 1992, conditions had not improved, as more evidence was coming to the public's attention that indicated a cover-up at Dow Corning. The FDA asked Dow Corning to release all its files and the company response was to hire former U.S. Attorney General Griffin Bell to do an independent audit of the entire matter. The company was seeking to give an ethical, objective response, but the investigation ultimately proved to be of little use to the company in restoring its reputation for moral integrity. Bell essentially cleared the company of mortal sins, and the company lawyers used the report to bolster its defense. But because the contents of the report remained sealed, critics charged that the company was engaged in another coverup. What had begun as an honest attempt to protect the employees interviewed by Bell and his team from questioning by aggressive plaintiff attorneys and the press had backfired.

Did new leadership work? In 1992, the board was getting restless. It threw out the chairman and the CEO and appointed Keith McKennon of Dow Chemical as CEO, hoping this would get the company back on track. One month later, McKennon took a first step, announcing that Dow Corning was no longer in the breast implant business.

But the damage was done. Losses mounted. In 1993, McKennon left. By 1995, Dow Corning had sought bankruptcy protection and, as tort lawyers continued to push litigation, the company began reexamining its commitment to manufacturing other medical products.

The Verdict

Was Dow Corning a company with solid ethics programs and committees that failed when they were most needed? Or was it a company that walked the narrow path but stayed atop the ethical edge even while making tough decisions and being unfairly criticized on all sides?

Was Dow Corning asleep at the switch, unprepared to handle an ethical, legal, and public relations crisis over one of its products? Or is it asking too much to expect any organization to be prepared for what Dow Corning faced?

Did Dow Corning rely too heavily on the advice of its lawyers, perhaps concluding that the silicone breast implant controversy was a legal battle fought between aggressive tort lawyers and one that would be won or lost in the courts? Or did they understand throughout the controversy that ethical and legal issues were involved and did they deal with both as best they could?

Was Dow Corning a victim of its own success, targeted unfairly as the major manufacturer of silicone implants, when in fact there were more than 60 manufacturers ultimately included in the settlement fund? Could Dow Corning have survived the controversy by immediately seeking to develop an industry-wide solution, involving physicians, attorneys, regulators, other companies and ethicists?

Was Dow Corning a victim of the nation's tort liability system, a stunning example of what can happen to any company with assets—no matter how ethical—which ventures into the inherently dangerous business of manufacturing medical products?

Did Dow Corning's ethics program and open culture work superbly well in the face of a sudden onslaught of problems, controversy, and difficult decisions? John Swanson, the former Dow Corning executive, now believes that the company acted unethically through much of the crisis.

Dow Corning declines to push one person out front to debate these issues—insisting that this would violate its own principle that all 8,300 employees have an equal ethics voice, and that they all speak for the company. It is for this very reason that members of the CCC rotate, with representation from Europe, Asia, the

United States, and elsewhere, and it is for this reason that its ethical standards do not vary from product to product or country to country. Dow Corning strives, it says, to achieve one ethical level: the highest.

Evaluating whether Dow Corning has achieved that goal is a challenge, because the very act of balancing competing ethical claims is always difficult. Understanding any company's ethical decision-making process and its results, whether contemporaneously or after the fact, is never easy. What is left is a kaleidoscope of images. The images change, they appear different to different people, but in the end we must all ask what we would have done if we had been there. What would have been the principled stand we would have taken?

Ethical decisions are rarely easy. They are sometimes unpopular. They usually don't satisfy everyone. And in a tale as complex as the Dow Corning story, there may never be agreement about what the right answer is.

12

NORTHROP CORPORATION
CLOSE ENOUGH

A Life of Its Own

The roots of what went wrong at Northrop Corporation can be traced to Norwood, Mass., and to what was then called Northrop's Precision Products Division (PPD). Located 20 miles from Boston, the division designed and manufactured gyroscopes and guidance systems for military and space applications. To quickly handle repairs and other service matters for its big West Coast customers, in the 1970s PPD set up a West Coast service department in Pomona, Calif. At the time of the incident, there were approximately 30 employees at Pomona out of a total of 46,000 throughout all of Northrop.

Pomona soon began submitting its own bids for new defense contracts. Gradually the West Coast operation began to take on a life of its own, with the managers back at Norwood allowing it to happen. In some ways Pomona's additional autonomy made sense because it could respond quickly to the needs of the West Coast customers in a way that Norwood couldn't. In retrospect, however, this was the beginning of the problems. More autonomy for

Pomona meant a loss of control and oversight for Norwood and for corporate headquarters. Thinking back, one manager remembered that Pomona's proposals were "very competitive. It seemed they were able to offer customized designs, with low up-front engineering costs, they were able to offer cheap qualification tests, they were able to offer extensive data requirements with no charge, they were able to meet fast delivery at low price. It was like a dream come true for the customers."

Red flags should have gone up, but they didn't. No one at the time said what should have been said: "If something looks that good, and if things are that cheap, and if they're making so much more money than anyone else, there has to be something wrong."

Pomona won contracts for the flight data transmitter for the air-launched cruise missile and a rate sensor assembly for the AV-8B Harrier Jump Jet that helped stabilize the plane during its vertical takeoffs.

Before shipping, all of the products were required to undergo extensive, contract-specified tests. A key test for the Harrier Jump Jet's rate sensor assembly was a vibration test that was designed to submit the sensitive gyroscope inside the unit to a force of up to 19 "Gs", or 19 times the force of gravity. Tests for the cruise missile's flight data transmitters involved putting the units through a cycle of strenuous vibration, as well as humidity and temperature extremes, to ensure that it could perform under the worst possible conditions.

These tests were vitally important, especially given the nature of the product. As one Northrop manager noted: "When you're making products that are being used in systems that carry nuclear weapons, you have to have...quality assurance systems, management oversight, technical competence, and adequate test equipment; these are givens." Unfortunately these "givens" were not in place for some of the products on these two Pomona programs.

What Went Wrong?

In June of 1987, Northrop executives were alarmed to learn that there had been serious irregularities in the testing of cruise missile components. They were not aware of the problems until the visit from the team of FBI investigators. The FBI had begun its investigation as the result of an anonymous tip.

By 1989, federal indictments were handed down charging 11 individuals and Northrop Corporation itself with 189 counts of fraud and conspiracy. What had happened?

In Pomona, the equipment used to test the cruise missile components occasionally malfunctioned. When this happened, a printout from a unit that had already passed its tests was substituted in the package with the untested unit. Pomona was essentially assuring its customers that the untested unit had passed the tests shown on the printout. In addition, Pomona managers and engineers cut other corners. For example, they decided not to inspect 34 of the units.

During the investigation, Pomona's chief engineer gave more bad news to the manager sent from Norwood. As the manager recalls: "The next morning he told me that there was another problem I should know about.... The vibration testing on the AV-8B Harrier Jump Jet rate sensor assembly had not been done correctly and in fact we were falsifying the vibration levels."

It turned out that the testing equipment at Pomona was incapable of reaching the required testing levels of 19Gs. The engineer said he was pressured into finding a way to get the tests done on the inadequate equipment. According to a manager who was later brought in to review the incident, the engineer "got very creative and was able to adjust the equipment to automatically falsify the calibration of the machine so that it would look like it was testing at 19Gs, but actually it was much less."

There were other problems as well. Fluid in the cruise missile gyroscopes was supposed to remain in a liquid state at temperatures far below zero. Some Northrop managers and engineers decided that this contract specification went too far. Although they knew that the fluid would freeze at the specified temperature, they decided that because of the heat in the missiles, the temperature would not reach that level of cold—no matter what the outside temperature. Rather than try to change the contract requirements, they instead alleged that all specifications were met.

The acts of commission at Pomona and omission at Norwood produced a number of serious consequences. Kent Kresa, the chairman, president and CEO, recalls the company's first reaction: "We recognized the severity of the criminal allegations against the company and immediately were in a defense mode in a legal sense, which was important in a way to protect the corporation and to protect individuals. But at the same time it hindered the ability of managers to just go in and look at the situation and perhaps change what we were doing."

Despite the roadblocks, Northrop's initial steps were decisive:

● The company launched an internal investigation to find out what had happened in its own ranks.

- The company informed its customers.
- People who were involved in the test fraud in Pomona were fired, and
- The entire operation at Pomona was shut down.

At the same time Northrop was addressing problems internally, the U.S. Congress was holding hearings on the incident. Eventually the Pomona general manager and the chief engineer went to prison, the government suspended the Norwood division from doing any new business with the government for two years, and consequently hundreds of Northrop employees lost their jobs.

In 1990, the company paid a $17 million fine for 34 testing irregularities. The government dropped the remaining charges and Northrop agreed to replace the fluid in the cruise missile gyroscopes to meet the original specifications.

"How Could This Happen Here?"

When the wrongdoing came to light, other Northrop employees reacted with anger. They were upset that so few affected "all of us." Many said they could not understand how the Pomona managers and engineers could bend the rules, take the risks, and do what they did. Kent Kresa correctly noted that this wasn't a case of a few "rotten apples." He recognized that what happened in Pomona "could occur somewhere else in the organization and that it could be a problem in the future if we don't stamp it out.... I don't think we should blame it on it being a small organization out away from the parent, I think we have to blame our own process."

Investigators agreed with Kresa. Col. Robert Allen of the

U.S. Air Force Defense Logistic Agency, Suspension Review Team, commented on the topic of corporate oversight:

"This is where we found errors principally of management, not so much of employees not being concerned about ethical conduct but [the failure of the] management system to open these up, bring them to light, to cross-feed them between the various divisions... there did not appear to be a systematic approach to exchanging information within the corporation. The corporation, in our view, was a series of very separate and distinct divisions that had very little interaction between each other."

Northrop's internal review pointed to several specific causes:

- An organization was established in which there were few checks and balances.

- There was a clear tension between resources and goals. The testing equipment was almost 20 years old and not adequate for the program, even when modified. As one manager said: "They didn't put any capital in there. This made them lean, mean and competitive; they were living on a shoestring. Now as we look at that test equipment, the stuff was held together with baling wire... then you couple that with their goals, for profit, for meeting sales... you have this situation where they became frantic. They couldn't attain their goals...."

- There was a closed-in environment at Pomona. According to Northrop managers: "If someone felt uncomfortable, we never got an opportunity to talk with that person... the environment was such that they weren't encouraged to come forward; in fact they may have even felt threatened."

Paying Close Attention

At the time of the incident, Northrop was in the process of revamping its ethics program in response to the requirements of the Defense Industry Initiative (DII). Northrop had been a charter signatory to the DII, a self-governance program that emerged from a commission on procurement appointed by President Ronald Reagan. These commitments by Northrop to ethics, compliance and quality assurance were reinforced in the wake of the Pomona case. Northrop also engaged employees in arriving at a consensus throughout the company on a set of commonly held values (see text, page 150).

The values then became basic to the program as it embraced compliance and moved beyond it to emphasize the role of values in ethical behavior and the need for leaders to apply the values in the workplace.

The goals of the program and the steps that have been taken at Northrop since 1987 are summed up in its "Ethics and Business Conduct Plan, 1995." This is reproduced in full on pages 152-53.

The approach to ensuring that employees understand and meet their ethical responsibilities has been to concentrate on training that develops leaders who are sensitive to ethical issues and ethical danger signs and who know how to support employees and allow them to "do the right thing." As Frank Daly, corporate director of ethics and business conduct, has said, "We aren't in the business of teaching people how to be ethical, we're teaching ethical people how to make a good decision when it could be difficult."

Northrop Grumman: Values From "Standard of Business Conduct"

We, the women and men of Northrop Grumman, are guided by the following Values. They describe our company as we want it to be. We want our decisions and actions to demonstrate these Values. We believe that putting our Values into practice creates long-term benefits for shareholders, customers, employees, suppliers, and the communities we serve.

We take responsibility for QUALITY...
Our products and services will be "best in class" in terms of value received for dollars paid. We will deliver excellence, strive for continuous improvement and respond vigorously to change. Each of us is responsible for the quality of whatever we do.

We deliver CUSTOMER SATISFACTION...
We are dedicated to satisfying our customers. We believe in respecting our customers, listening to their requests and understanding their expectations. We strive to exceed their expectations in affordability, quality and on-time delivery.

We provide LEADERSHIP as a company and as individuals...
Northrop Grumman's leadership is founded on talented employees effectively applying advanced technology, innovative manufacturing and sound business management. We add more value at lower cost with faster response. We each lead through our competence. creativity and teamwork.

We act with INTEGRITY in all we do...
We are each personally accountable for the highest standards of behavior, including honesty and fairness in all aspects of our work. We fulfill our commitments as responsible citizens and employees. We will consistently treat customers and company resources with the respect they deserve.

We value Northrop Grumman PEOPLE...
We treat one another with respect and take pride in the significant contributions that come from the diversity of individuals and ideas. Our continued success requires us to provide the education and development needed to help our people grow. We are committed to openness and trust in all relationships.

We regard our SUPPLIERS as essential team members...
We owe our suppliers the same type of respect that we show to our customers. Our suppliers deserve fair and equitable treatment, clear agreements and honest feedback on performance. We consider our suppliers' needs in conducting all aspects of our business.

Making the right decision can be more difficult when the day-to-day pressures of the job build to a breaking point. People are often unwilling to say they can't do the job, and so instead they bend the rules. A key lesson learned from the Pomona incident is that keeping to tight manufacturing schedules set against a backdrop of unrealistic projected goals can directly lead to cutting corners, avoiding tough questions, and eventually unethical and illegal behavior. Shirley Peterson, corporate vice president of organization development and ethics, said, "We learned as we went out and talked to our people that the environment we work in and the pressures of the schedule are very heavy. You can easily allow that to cause an imbalance in the importance you place on quality."

Addressing this problem begins with reevaluating how leadership is defined within the organization. Everyone at Northrop is exposed regularly to the company's values and ethical business practices through a series of training sessions and other communication techniques. The goal is to give each person "an internalized guide to behavior on the job." One example of these sessions is the Management Leadership Conference, which Peterson describes as an opportunity for managers to "come together and talk about the elements of being a leader and how you build problem-solving teams." The participants discuss leadership conflict, they role-play, and in the end they evaluate each other's abilities.

This is one of the most innovative ethics initiatives at Northrop. Called "The Northrop Leadership Inventory," it is a checklist of behavioral characteristics tied to the Northrop values. They have a direct bearing on the way leaders shape the ethical

Putting Shared Values into Action

Goals	Strategies
1 Create a common employee understanding of the role of values and business conduct in guiding the corporation	• Encourage the proactive commitment and involvement of leadership establishing and demonstrating a values-driven environment at North Grumman • Position the corporate ethics office as a strategic partner • Clarify the guiding role of company values in motivating compliance achieving self-governance • Develop employee understanding of the importance of employee val and ethical standards while operating in a dynamic environment • Identify values and ethics as a certainty in uncertain times to guide employee actions in development of the corporation
2 Foster demonstration by all employees on a day-to-day basis that Northrop Grumman is a values-driven and ethical corporation	• Develop a values-based ethics message to be delivered by the CEO and executive (VP) team in communications • Develop and implement ongoing education program and initiatives o Ethics & Business Conduct • Promote the use of Northrop Grumman Standards of Business Conc as a key resource to guide ethical decision-making • Implement a communications plan to improve employee understand of Northrop Grumman Ethics and Standards of Business Conduct
3 Increase consistency and quality standards in Ethics & Business Conduct program processes across the corporation	• Ensure consistency of approaches and interpretations among the Business Conduct Officers (BCOs) • Identify program processes that need improvement • Develop an internal evaluation methodology • Make senior management oversight more visible
4 Strengthen appreciation by internal and external audiences of the corporation's good name and values-driven approach	• Implement a focused proactive plan together with the leadership of corporation, public affairs and corporate communications to secure understanding and perception that Northrop Grumman is an ethical company

itiatives	Measures
Conduct Business Conduct Officer (BCO) training and regular discussions with management to assess integration and implementation of Ethics & Business Conduct program Hold Leadership Conferences and Leadership Inventory feedback for top 400 Northrop Grumman leaders Partner with other functions to support top 400 leaders in their personal leadership follow-up plan Produce a Values Information Kit for managers so they can lead flow-down discussions with employees Establish cross-functional work team to determine effectiveness of ethics component of the PMP Determine future use of High Integrity Environment pilot project	• Assess BCO role • Establish Leadership Inventory data as tool for individual/group progress • Surveys, focus groups • PMP ethics component
Conduct Ethics and Standards of Business Conduct training for all employees including use of new Standards of Business Conduct manual Develop and distribute an informational brochure for employees that describes the purpose of the Ethics & Business Conduct Office and the services offered Establish partnership with employee communications & public affairs functions to provide executive written/spoken messages on Values & Ethics Produce an "Ethics Quarterly" bulletin for all employees Team with the Law Department to present sessions to Site & Division management teams that raise sensitivity to compliance issues	• Division reports on employee participation in Standards of Business Conduct Training • OpenLine trend data • Observation of demonstrated actions • Annual ethics review and survey
Conduct regular BCO meetings and cross-feed best practices in program operations Design internal evaluation instrument, for example, peer review Implement interactive video compliance training at locations without this resource Periodic cross-feed of ethics cases and lessons learned Research computerization program and multiyear implementation schedule Corporate Policy Council approves annual plan and ongoing oversight	• Product delivery • System delivery • Commitment to process
Continue Best Practices discussions and interface with DoD and coordinate administrative agreement commitments CEO as keynote speaker at 1995 DII Forum VP, Corporate Ethics Office to make presentation at 1995 Conference Board National Ethics Conference Ongoing corporate office involvement in national Ethics Officer Association Accommodate assistance and information requests from other companies, educational institutions and professional journals	• External requests for assistance and information

environment. Each manager receives a summary of how others evaluated him or her.

After Peterson went through the process, she said, "I tell you, it really hits home. You think, this is how I am perceived; these are the messages my behavior sends to people I work with. And you see what you need to focus on to improve."

Each participant is next asked to identify the two or three behaviors he or she needs to address, and then is given whatever assistance is necessary to develop a "personal improvement plan." Several sections from the inventory are presented on pages 156-57.

Much has happened since the incident at Pomona and its aftermath. Most importantly, in 1994, Northrop, Grumman Corporation and Vought Aircraft became one entity: the Northrop Grumman Corporation. The transition was a challenge to management. They needed, among other things, to thread through the new organization a clear understanding of what principles and values they stood for, what ethical policies and procedures they deemed essential, and what they would not compromise about. The challenge was made more difficult because of past ethical and legal problems at Grumman that had reached the highest levels of the organization. A few years earlier, Grumman's chairman had been fired after reports of alleged irregularities involving loans from a supplier.

Kent Kresa, Northrop Grumman's leader, has tried to bring the message to each and every employee at Northrop Grumman that he or she should feel personally responsible for helping the company meet its ethics goals.

"Most important is the individual. You shouldn't look at

your job as a narrow little island," said Kresa. "You have a responsibility to the whole, to the whole corporation, for it to be successful. And the corporation has a relationship with you that if it is successful, you should be successful; so it's a common bond. That openness says that you will communicate your concerns, your best ideas, so that people should tend to want to operate in the right way, and if someone sees something that isn't being done that way, they will challenge it…. We try to encourage an environment where we depend on the operator on the line to come forward. That's my first line of defense."

To help employees make the tough calls, Northrop Grumman distributes guidelines that it calls "When to Challenge" and "When to Support." See pages 158–59 for text of these guidelines.

Northrop Grumman has created an integrated ethics, compliance, and quality assurance program and has designed a training and communication strategy that brings the message to each and every employee. It is difficult, of course, to maintain **the ethical edge** continually. Any system is only as good as the next challenge that comes along. But, in Kent Kresa's words, Northrop Grumman will face the next challenge in an "honest, straightforward and open way."

**Northrop Grumman: Sample Sections From
"The Northrop Leadership Inventory"**

ACKNOWLEDGING CONTRIBUTION

24. Listens to other people's ideas	HD	D	N	S	HS	NI
25. Works to see the value of others' opinions (even if they differ from his/her own)	HD	D	N	S	HS	NI
26. Personally recognizes performance improvement in others	HD	D	N	S	HS	NI
27. Effectively recognizes outstanding performance	HD	D	N	S	HS	NI
28. Gives people the authority they need to do their job	HD	D	N	S	HS	NI
29. Gives people the freedom they need to do their job	HD	D	N	S	HS	NI

SUPPLIERS
Working with Suppliers

30. Shows respect for suppliers as team members	HD	D	N	S	HS	NI
31. Insists on high standards of performance from suppliers	HD	D	N	S	HS	NI
32. Recognizes the needs of suppliers	HD	D	N	S	HS	NI
33. Values the contributions of suppliers	HD	D	N	S	HS	NI
34. Works well with suppliers	HD	D	N	S	HS	NI

QUALITY
Achieving Excellence

35. Makes sure individual objectives are clearly understood	HD	D	N	S	HS	NI
36. Insists on high standards of performance	HD	D	N	S	HS	NI
37. Strives to be the best at whatever she/he does	HD	D	N	S	HS	NI
38. Challenges others to be the best they can be	HD	D	N	S	HS	NI
39. Is willing to challenge the system to achieve quality results	HD	D	N	S	HS	NI
40. Defines quality as meeting customer needs, including cost and schedule	HD	D	N	S	HS	NI
41. Makes Total Quality Management part of day-to-day work processes	HD	D	N	S	HS	NI

Continuous Improvement

42. Asks people what they need to do their work better	HD	D	N	S	HS	NI
43. Involves others in continuous process improvement	HD	D	N	S	HS	NI
44. Effectively deals with performance problems	HD	D	N	S	HS	NI
45. Strives to improve others' performance from acceptable to excellent	HD	D	N	S	HS	NI
46. Encourages creativity in others	HD	D	N	S	HS	NI
47. Takes appropriate risks in letting others try out new ideas	HD	D	N	S	HS	NI

INTEGRITY
Corporate Citizenship

48. Represents Northrop in a positive manner when dealing with external constituencies	HD	D	N	S	HS	NI
49. Is supportive of community activities	HD	D	N	S	HS	NI

50. Avoids both the perception and the reality of fraud, waste,or abuse   HD   D   N   S   HS   NI

51. Communicates the importance of personal safety   HD   D   N   S   HS   NI

52. Considers environmental impact of actions and decisions   HD   D   N   S   HS   NI

Business Integrity

53. Demonstrates honesty and good ethical behavior in all business transactions   HD   D   N   S   HS   NI

54. Confronts and deals with integrity issues   HD   D   N   S   HS   NI

55. Ensures that company and professional standards are fairly applied   HD   D   N   S   HS   NI

56. Avoids "playing favorites"   HD   D   N   S   HS   NI

57. Ensures honest reporting of budget reports, projections, and results   HD   D   N   S   HS   NI

58. Encourages individuals to surface concerns quickly and honestly (doesn't "shoot the messenger)   HD   D   N   S   HS   NI

Personal Integrity

59. Shows a high degree of personal integrity in dealing with others   HD   D   N   S   HS   NI

60. Stands up for what she/he believes in (even under pressure)   HD   D   N   S   HS   NI

61. Consistently does what is "right" as opposed to what is "expedient"   HD   D   N   S   HS   NI

62. Leads by example   HD   D   N   S   HS   NI

LEADERSHIP

Corporate Leadership

63. Inspires pride in Northrop   HD   D   N   S   HS   NI

64. Communicates and supports Northrop's mission   HD   D   N   S   HS   NI

65. Demonstrates a personal commitment to increasing Northrop's profitability   HD   D   N   S   HS   NI

66. Seeks ways to eliminate unnecessary expense   HD   D   N   S   HS   NI

67. Works effectively with people outside her/his group to get the job done   HD   D   N   S   HS   NI

68. Communicates the importance of Northrop's contributions to ourcountry   HD   D   N   S   HS   NI

Team Leadership

69. Encourages individuals to work together as a team   HD   D   N   S   HS   NI

70. Treats others in Northrop as colleagues, not as competitors   HD   D   N   S   HS   NI

71. Communicates a clear vision of his/her team's direction   HD   D   N   S   HS   NI

72. Takes personal responsibility for helping to make sure the team achieves its goals   HD   D   N   S   HS   NI

73. Creates an environment where the team feels responsible for its own success or failure   HD   D   N   S   HS   NI

HD = Highly Dissatisfied; D = Dissatisfied; N = Neither Satisfied nor Dissatisfied; S = Satisfied; HS = Highly Satisfied; NI = No Information

Northrop Grumman:
"When to Challenge" and
"When to Support" Guidelines

WHEN TO CHALLENGE

LIVING NORTHROP VALUES

If you are ever asked to do something which you believe is either unethical or not in Northrop's best interest, or if you become aware of any such activities ... it is not only your right to express your concerns, it is your responsibilities.

Your responsibilities: 1) raise your concerns in a timely manner; 2) be constructive and positive; 3) listen to your manager's response 4) accept that you may have to "agree to disagree."

Your management's responsibilities: 1) encourage communication 2) listen to your concerns 3) allow you to express your opinions 4) respect that you cared enough to express your concerns.

GUIDELINES FOR CHALLENGING

1. Volunteer information any time you believe you can help better achieve our objectives. This could include early warnings on program cost, schedule, or technical performance, or suggestions to improve processes. Put yourself in your manager's position and provide the information you would want if you were in his or her shoes. Don't assume your management is aware of the problem, has all the information, or already shares your concerns.

2. If you are ever asked to do something that you believe is illegal or unethical, express your concern to your manager immediately. It may be appropriate to take the matter "up the chain of command," making higher levels aware of the situation. If you feel the matter requires another approach, you have several options. You may contact any of the following:
   a) your Business Practices Administrator;
   b) Employee Relations;
   c) the Security office at your location;
   d) legal counsel at your location;
   e) the corporate Business Practices Open Line (800/247-4952).

3. If you are asked to do something legal and ethical, but which, for some other reason, you believe is not in Northrop's best interest: a) Express your concern to your manager in a timely manner. Where possible, do so in a private meeting. b) Let your manager know why you feel your instructions are not in Northrop's best interest. c) If possible, communicate an alternative strategy that you feel may be more beneficial. d) Be open to realize that others may disagree with your opinion and that this may be an issue of business judgment, not a matter of right or wrong. e) Avoid griping or complaining to co-workers.

4. Remember, once you reach a final decision and a final decision is made, the emphasis moves from CHALLENGING to SUPPORTING. Decisions may reflect the fact that your management has different information or a different perspective than you do.

NORTHROP

WHEN TO CHALLENGE

LIVING NORTHROP VALUES

If you are ever asked to do something which you believe is either unethical or not in Northrop's best interest, or if you become aware of any such activities ... it is not only your right to express your concerns, it is your responsibilities.

Your responsibilities: 1) raise your concerns in a timely manner; 2) be constructive and positive; 3) listen to your manager's response; 4) accept that you may have to "agree to disagree."

Your management's responsibilities: 1) encourage communication; 2) listen to your concerns; 3) allow you to express your opinions 4) respect that you cared enough to express your concerns.

GUIDELINES FOR CHALLENGING

1. Volunteer information any time you believe you can help better achieve our objectives. This could include early warnings on program cost, schedule, or technical performance, or suggestions to improve processes. Put yourself in your manager's position and provide the information you would want if you were in his or her shoes. Don't assume your management is aware of the problem, has all the information, or already shares your concerns.

2. If you are ever asked to do something that you believe is illegal or unethical, express your concern to your manager immediately. It may be appropriate to take the matter "up the chain of command," making higher levels aware of the situation. If you feel the matter requires another approach, you have several options. You may contact any of the following: a) your Business Practices Administrator; b) Employee Relations; c) the Security office at your location; d) legal counsel at your location; e) the corporate Business Practices Open Line (800/247-4952).

3. If you are asked to do something legal and ethical, but which, for some other reason, you believe is not in Northrop's best interest: a) Express your concern to your manager in a timely manner. Where possible, do so in a private meeting. b) Let your manager know why you feel your instructions are not in Northrop's best interest. c) If possible, communicate an alternative strategy that you feel may be more beneficial. d) Be open to realize that others may disagree with your opinion and that this may be an issue of business judgment, not a matter of right or wrong. e) Avoid griping or complaining to co-workers.

4. Remember, once your concern has been heard and a final decision is made, the emphasis moves from CHALLENGING to SUPPORTING. Decisions may reflect the fact that your management has different information or a different perspective than you do.

WHEN TO SUPPORT

LIVING NORTHROP VALUES

Each of us needs to realize that we are responsible for the external and internal image of our corporation. We should build pride in Northrop wherever we can, and support our team as best we can.

SUPPORTING Northrop involves taking the responsibility for decisions once they are made, without "passing the buck" or blaming others.

Your responsibilities:

    1) do your best to successfully carry out final decisions

    2) explain the reasons for decisions to other involved co-workers.

Your management's responsibilities:

    1) take the time to explain decisions so that you understand the rationale and logic behind them

    2) *listen* to your questions and concerns

    3) *coach* on how best to implement final decisions.

GUIDELINES FOR SUPPORTING

1. Take responsibility for what you say and do. Avoid "buck passing" remarks like *"They* told me to tell you this." or "This was *their* idea."

2. Avoid "bad-mouthing" others. If you disagree, use the "WHEN TO CHALLENGE" philosophy, and discuss the issue in a responsible and constructive manner.

3. Take the time to explain decisions to people. "Add value" by discussing the reasons for decisions, and the significance of the action at your level in the organization.

"Think before you speak" is a universal rule—especially when practicing this CHALLENGE and SUPPORT philosophy.

Use NORTHROP's VALUES as guideposts. Will your words and actions help to:

- satisfy our **Customers?**
- support **Northrop People?**
- assist **Suppliers?**
- improve **Quality?**
- demonstrate **Integrity?**
- provide **Leadership?**

When the answers are "Yes," we're moving in the right direction.

13

MORE TALES OF "WHEN ENOUGH WAS NOT ENOUGH

GENERAL ELECTRIC, AND THE BODY COMPANY

Whistle-blowers or Bounty Hunters?

From time to time during the U.S. Civil War, President Abraham Lincoln received reports that soldiers on the battle lines had opened kegs of what they thought was gunpowder, only to discover that they instead contained sawdust. Cavalry officers reported that boots were wearing thin in a matter of days; when confronted, the manufacturer acted surprised, saying, "I didn't think the cavalry would be doing much walking."

These and other instances of shoddy or faulty products prompted Lincoln to push for the False Claims Act of 1863. The law stated that employees of arms manufacturers and other government contractors have a duty to "blow the whistle" if they had information indicating that harm to the national interest was likely. Despite promises of protection under the law, retaliation against whistle-blowers was nevertheless still commonplace.

For the next century, support for whistle-blowing existed only during wartime. Even then, it existed only if the whistle-blowing was directly linked to the safety of the "boys at the front." Otherwise, the dominant opinion was that whistle-blowers were disloyal employees who disrupted business and destroyed reputations of good people and good companies.

During the 1970s, as the public paid more attention to corporate wrongdoing, the taboo against whistle-blowing began to fade, albeit very slowly. The emerging rule of thumb became: "Employees have a duty to blow the whistle if harm to a third party is likely."

This rule of thumb was a bit broader than the former "protect the boys at the front" principle. Still, it was expected that an employee would exhaust all possible internal channels to report wrongdoing and would blow the whistle externally only if there were no other options available. Furthermore, it was assumed that an employee who would blow the whistle would be motivated by pure principle, without any ulterior motives.

In 1986, however, the rules about whistle-blowing changed again. The False Claim Act of 1863 was dusted off and amended. It now encourages citizens to blow the whistle and bring lawsuits against companies that are defrauding the government. The new law, however, also creates incentives for whistle-blowers, who are now eligible to receive up to 25 percent of the monies recovered. Chester Walsh, a former employee of General Electric, is now a multimillionaire thanks to the new law.

From New Jersey Fronts to Middle East Intrigue

Beginning in 1986, a General Electric manager conspired with an

Israeli general to siphon off U.S. military aid funds. The money went in part to fund Israeli military programs that did not qualify for U.S. help; ultimately, at least $11 million ended up in a Swiss bank account that was controlled by the GE manager and the general. Some have speculated that this money was intended for future covert military operations, though this has never been proved.

In court papers, General Electric said that a number of its employees were aware of the illegal diversions, which were accomplished with phony vouchers issuing funds to a New Jersey front company. Some employees wondered why millions of dollars were going to a company that did not exist just a short time before. A GE spokesperson admitted that its "system should have caught them," but it didn't.

In 1992, General Electric pleaded guilty to charges of fraud, money laundering, and corrupt business practices and agreed to pay $69 million in fines and penalties. In all, 22 GE employees were either fired, forced to retire, demoted, or fined by the company.

The scheme might never have come to light if not for Chester Walsh, a General Electric marketing executive in Israel. Over a five-year period, Walsh smuggled documents out of Israel, secretly recorded conversations, and gathered evidence of the fraud. Eventually, his attorneys and a nonprofit organization, Taxpayers Against Fraud, filed suit. Under the False Claims Act, Walsh and the nonprofit split an $11.5 million award.

General Electric and the U.S. Department of Justice argued that Walsh "manipulated" the whistle-blower protection act by delaying his lawsuit for several years, thereby increasing the final bounty. They sought to have the court of appeals reduce the

award. The court disagreed and sharply criticized GE and the
Department of Justice. Walsh argued that he delayed and did not
use GE's internal reporting system because he was afraid of retaliation. He cited one example of an employee who was reassigned
after reporting his suspicions.

To this day, Walsh's motives are a subject of much dispute.
General Electric representatives point to the extensive commitment it has made to ethics and compliance. They note that GE
was a principal force behind the Defense Industry Initiative and
that it has done everything a corporation can be expected to do to
detect and prevent wrongdoing. They point with pride to the company's corporatewide ombudsman program and to its ethics training initiatives. Critics of the False Claims Act argue that employees should at the very least be required to attempt to use internal
mechanisms when they are available. This is especially true if the
whistle-blower stands to gain financially by not using the internal
system.

More and more organizations are rolling out ethics codes
and creating internal "helpline" reporting systems. Unfortunately,
some of these organizations are not making the additional long-
term commitment to ethics training and to taking the further
steps that are necessary to build an ethical culture, among which
are changes in incentive and bonus plans, inclusion of ethics in
performance appraisals, building ethical consideration into the
business planning process, and most importantly supporting
employees in their efforts to be ethical on the job. Companies that
only go partway are creating the conditions for a repeat of the
Chester Walsh case. Their employees are more aware than ever

before of the importance of ethics; they know that their company has a code and an internal reporting system, but they also know that the corporate culture has largely been unchanged.

Changing a corporate culture to alleviate these fears is no easy matter. In fact, it is the single toughest task facing ethics officers. It takes but one incident of retaliation in the face of efforts to prevent it, and the ethics initiative is back to square one.

There's no quick fix to the "whistle-blower or bounty hunter" dilemma. Legislative solutions are possible, and several U.S. states have enacted whistle-blower protection laws that require employees to use internal systems whenever possible. Monetary incentives will continue to be necessary, however, as long as employees have legitimate reasons to fear retaliation if they "blow the whistle." And, although unfortunate but in many cases true, it may take incentives to prompt people to go the extra mile, run the risks, and report wrongdoing.

The Body Shop and its "Shattered Image"

For some, "business ethics" is synonymous with a small group of companies that have been identified as being "socially responsible" and "green." The Body Shop and Ben & Jerry's Ice Cream are perhaps the best known examples of such companies. These and other like-minded enterprises are seen as representing a new breed of capitalism. Contrary to the "business as usual" approach, these companies actively promote social goals. The founders and their representatives operate the businesses with special sensitivity to the environment, to the interests of indigenous people, to animal rights, and to other similar causes.

A cottage industry has sprung up around the "social respon-sibility" movement. The Businesses for Social Responsibility (BSR) organization has more than 800 member companies. Numerous newsletters, articles, and books focus on the topic. "Social respon-sibility" conferences are held regularly, financial advisers help "socially responsible" and "green" investors find companies that share their vision and personal values, and certain mutual funds invest only in companies that meet their responsibility criteria.

Recently the "social responsibility" movement has been shaken by allegations that some of its standard-bearer companies are more image than substance. In particular, critics have zeroed in on the Body Shop, the worldwide chain of retail stores selling cosmetics and personal care products. Others, in defense of the Body Shop, claim it is being unfairly attacked. They say that while it may have fallen short of its high ideals, it has always remained true to its principles. At any rate, defenders have now circled the wagons, launched counterattacks against the critics, and vowed to weather the storm for the sake of "the movement."

Is this in reality a case of "when enough was not enough"—an example of a company that has fallen short of its own high ideals? Or is it, as critic Jon Entine, an Emmy Award-winning investigative journalist maintains, a story not of a company that somehow lost its moral compass but "the tale of a business that never had one"?

Building an Image

The Body Shop empire began in 1976 when entrepreneur Anita Roddick opened a cosmetics shop in Brighton, England. Her early success was attributed to her promises that her products were "natural" and "100 percent pure." Her charismatic, irreverent personality also greatly contributed to the growth of her business. Roddick became a celebrity by regularly criticizing cosmetics makers as immoral frauds who "lie" and "cheat." Over time she became a feminist role model and a leader of a new, entrepreneurial, progressive type of capitalism.

The company's image grew along with hers. The Body Shop's products were marketed not only as "natural," but also as having been developed in cooperation with indigenous people who benefited from their sales through the Trade Not Aid program. As Roddick put it: "We see ourselves not just as a creator of profits for our shareholders, but as a force for good, working for the future of the planet.... Enlightened capitalism is the best way of changing society for the better. I think you can trade ethically, be committed to social responsibility, empower your employees without being afraid of them. I think you can rewrite the book on business."

Run by Roddick and her husband, Gordon, Body Shop International (BSI) by 1995 had more than a thousand stores in 45 countries and annual worldwide sales in excess of $700 million.

The Image Is "Shattered"

In 1994, several highly critical magazine articles appeared. Among them was Jon Entine's article "Shattered Image," which appeared in *Business Ethics* magazine. Of the Body Shop and the Roddicks he made the following accusations:

- The Body Shop invented stories about the exotic origins of some of its products, many of which were actually off-the-shelf product formulas containing nonrenewable petrochemicals and preservatives. One cosmetics expert was quoted, "It is not a very innovative company. Roddick uses petrochemically sourced ingredients... which some natural cosmetics companies have phased out." A competitor complained, "If you take the Body Shop name off the products and put 'Payless Drug Store' on the label, you get an idea of the products' quality."

- From 1986 to 1993 the Body Shop's charitable contributions were comparatively low despite the company claim that, "The Body Shop donates an inordinately high percentage of pretax profits to often controversial charitable campaigns."

- The Body Shop's Trade Not Aid initiative and its claim of "first-world wages for third-world products" is more a marketing gimmick than a business policy.

The article also pointed to quality control problems, to "abusive practices" toward its franchisees, and to strong-arm tactics against critics.

The Body Shop has countered Entine and other critics by questioning their sources, arguing that quotes were taken out of context, and threatening legal action. Entine has stood by his claims, challenged the "social responsibility" movement to look in the mirror, and has recently cautioned: "Oversimplifying complex moral issues and exaggerating positive corporate behavior will only breed cynicism in the end. This is a slippery slope and many otherwise ethical companies are sliding down it."

Social Responsibility and the Ethical Edge

The debate over the Body Shop will no doubt continue, with valid points made on each side. In any case the controversy raises serious problems about the relationship between business ethics and the notion of "socially responsible" companies.

The first and most obvious problem is that the "social responsibility" movement too often assumes that there is consensus as to how social responsibility is defined. So far the movement has embraced companies that are known for their quality of work life programs, environmentalism, and/or local community service initiatives. More controversial, however, are some of the additional litmus tests that are popular among social investors, including proscriptions against tobacco, alcohol, and arms manufacturers, and support of "reproductive rights." To date, the movement has not embraced any items from the social agenda of the more politically conservative end of the spectrum. Critics have argued that this implies selective morality. To some, record companies with "gangsta rap" labels may not be any more socially responsible than tobacco manufacturers.

It hardly seems that there is a consensus about what a "socially responsible" company should be responsible for. This is, of course, not a problem if we are talking about employees, customers, investors, and others who knowingly choose to support a company that shares their set of values. It becomes a problem, however, if companies misrepresent their values and/or turn out to be more image than reality. And it becomes a more widespread problem if business ethics becomes widely identified or synonymous with such companies.

Regardless of which set of values "socially responsible" companies ultimately endorse, the overall approach seems to rest on what is called the "stakeholder theory." This theory argues that businesses should act in the interests of all *stake*holders and not just in the interests of *stock*holders. One of the difficulties with this theory, however, is that it has never been very helpful in prioritizing competing demands. For example, examine the following dilemmas:

- Is a company "socially responsible" if it lays off employees rather than scaling back its support for local charities?

- How should a corporation spend its resources in difficult times? Should it go ahead with its diversity training initiative? Conduct an additional environmental compliance audit? Create a worker retraining program to soften the blow of impending layoffs? Continue its restoration projects in the Amazon basin? Or should it do none of the above and instead concentrate its resources on increasing sales?

- If a company can increase its profits and donate more money to charity by moving its manufacturing plants overseas, should it do so?

- Which set of stakeholders takes precedence? If the company chooses to concentrate on increasing sales or profits, does that mean it is no longer "socially responsible"?

Finally, too often the "social responsibility" movement has ignored the importance of internal ethics and compliance controls. Instead, proponents have focused almost entirely on external corporate relations. Companies are often praised for their values statements and support of popular causes even though they may have no internal procedures to either ensure that the values are lived up to, or to help employees make difficult choices when values conflict. Far too frequently the "social responsibility" movement has ignored companies like those that have gained the ethical edge by quietly making significant efforts to integrate ethics into their daily operations through training, changes in performance appraisals, "helplines," and ethics offices.

The "social responsibility" movement is based on the praiseworthy goal of promoting business ethics. Unfortunately, it can have the effect of setting back business ethics by diverting attention from more thoughtful and practical approaches, and by providing an easy target for those critics who believe that business ethicists are well-meaning but naive "do-gooders" with a specific social agenda.

Good Intentions Are Not Enough
The Hazards of Hotlines, Whistle-blowers, and Investigations

The Target

You are the ethics officer at Marcher Adlins, a worldwide manufacturing firm. You have just installed an ethics "hotline," a 24-hour-a-day 1-800-number that allows employees to report instances of possible ethical violations. Yesterday, an anonymous call was made to the company's hotline by a caller accusing a distinguished senior purchasing executive of being involved in a kickback scheme. You suspect the accusation to be false. Nevertheless, the caller gives details, sounds knowledgeable and appears to be on the level.

Based on the phone call, you launch an investigation involving staff from human resources, corporate counsel, purchasing, accounting, and security. The executive's name is never mentioned to his coworkers, but from the questions being asked of them, he discovers in short order that he is a suspect. Finally, you call him in for questioning; you do not tell him that an investigation is under way; you do not "Mirandize" him before questioning, nor do you allow him to face his accuser. He tells you he cannot sleep at night and does not know what to do or where to turn. Furthermore, while he was an enthusiastic supporter of the company's expanding ethics initiatives, including its new hotline, he informs you that, in view of what has happened to him, he is not so sure it was a good idea.

Was it a good idea?

There are hazards in such devices as hotlines (also called helplines or guidelines) and other initiatives that encourage anonymous tips. Investigations that impinge upon individual rights are often conducted in the name of ethics without due process and without any protection for the rights of the accused. Furthermore, such "anonymous tip" mechanisms may make it easier to register false accusations.

There is little doubt that corporations and employees who take the initiative to install hotlines have good intentions. Corporations want to make ethics part of their ongoing operations; individuals want to do the right thing. Are good intentions good enough, though? We say they are not. Serious consequences must be taken into account in initiating ethics programs. The above case and the following ones on hotlines, whistle-blowers, and investigations have elicited different answers to the handling of such consequences. Which one is right, or do they both have important points to make?

Answer One

Ethics initiatives must prevail over individual rights. Taking the protections of individual rights afforded to citizens and extending them to the workplace is an interesting theoretical idea to contemplate. Unfortunately, it simply can't be done. It is inefficient and unworkable, and would achieve no more than the creation of an overly legalistic and confrontational environment. Employees do not have a right to employment or due process. Specific rights and due process may be bargained for and made part of contractual agreements, but in the absence of an explicit contract or provable acts of discrimination, an employer is generally free to investigate situations and terminate an employee at will. In short, though it may not be perfect, the employment-at-will doctrine is a necessary condition for business efficiency and productivity. Therefore, on that basis, it is justifiable to limit employee rights and due process. Ethics can go only so far in business.

Answer Two

The pursuit of ethical ideas must never be undertaken in a way that abuses individual rights in an unethical manner. As a general principle, it is more ethical to respect individual rights and due process than to trample them. Some companies have instituted programs that meet the practical demands of business while maintaining a respect for due process. If these companies can design programs that work, others can follow their model. To do otherwise is shortsighted. There is a clear alternative, and the damaged reputations from anonymous calls are not a price worth paying in the name of ethics.

The Protector

You are the ethics officer at Marcher Adlins, a worldwide manufacturing firm. In the past two years, thanks to a whistle-blower

Hotline Hints

Lockheed-Martin executives have implemented a hotline approach that works. They argue that what is needed is not anonymity but a form of "witness protection." Callers to their helpline are required to state their name, but this information is not included in any further documentation. In most cases, the caller's identity is known only to the ethics officer. This is a simple way of drastically reducing the number of false accusations without impairing the efficacy of the ethics hotline.

A second technique that has been successful at some corporations is to notify the accused except when there are extenuating circumstances. This places the burden of proof on the investigators to explain why notification should not occur. In cases where notification would clearly hamper the investigation, however, the option to withhold notification remains open.

whose identity you know, your office has uncovered massive fraud in the purchasing department. Executives were fired and an independent board investigation resulted in top-to-bottom scrutiny of the entire company. Even the Department of Justice has initiated an investigation of wrongdoing. You know for a fact that divisions will be sold and extensive downsizing of the company awaits up the road. Now your whistle-blower has called you to say he expects to receive preferential treatment when the company downsizes.

Should you protect him?

Answer One

It is difficult and potentially costly to prove that a former whistle-blower is not being laid off in retaliation for his actions. It is easier to transfer him or otherwise protect him from being dismissed.

Answer Two

If the whistle-blower is protected, someone who otherwise would have kept his or her job may be laid off in the whistle-blower's place. This result is unethical and could have been avoided if there were sufficient documentation both at the time of the whistle-blowing incident and during the downsizing.

The Payoff

You are the ethics officer at Marcher Adlins, a worldwide manufacturing firm that has experienced widespread ethical abuses, government investigations, and negative publicity. The ethics committee of the board of directors has now instructed you to institute a companywide "ethics award system" modeled on the federal whistle-blower protection law. In other words, the company will be providing a financial reward to whistle-blowers (figured as a percentage based on the amount of the fraud) if there is a successful federal prosecution.

Should you do it?

Answer One

Go along with the ethics committee of the board. As long as the federal government has financial incentives for external whistle-blowing, corporations must provide such incentives inside the company to try and prevent employees from going outside.

Human nature being what it is, whistle-blowers will be attracted to the money; furthermore, many people might not report wrong-doing at all without some kind of incentives.

Answer Two

Your job is to guide the board and, as a member of the Ethics Officer Association, you've learned from your peers that there are hidden hazards in such bounty provisions of whistle-blowing pro-grams. First, they provide an incentive to the employee to wait while the fraud grows before blowing the whistle externally to receive a larger bounty. Second, a companywide ethics award sys-tem actually encourages bounty-hunting, contributing to false claims and possible collusion with wrongdoers. Third, such an award system is really counter to what ethics is all about—doing what's right for its own sake.

Whose Call

You are the ethics officer at Marcher Adlins, a worldwide manu-facturing firm. You have decided to implement an ethics helpline, a 24-hour-a-day 1-800-number that allows employees to ask ques-tions about ethical issues or potential violations. Because you are busy handling investigations, you will train your staff to answer questions based on a detailed code of compliance you will write, yet you remain troubled. One of the missions of your ethics pro-gram is to instill ethical decision making throughout the company.

Should you implement the helpline?

Answer One

As past crises have demonstrated, ethical decision making is too important to be left to local managers. The costs are simply too high and, now that scrutiny has heightened, the company cannot afford any more mistakes. You worked hard to develop the code of compliance, and a helpline is just the final step needed to ensure that the program works. This way there can be absolutely no doubt about what the code requires.

Answer Two

Ethical decision making must be local and decentralized, and decision makers should be encouraged to be ethically reflective. The helpline can be a backup, but ethics administrators recognize that for such programs to be successful, decentralization must be coupled with genuine autonomy and a corporate trust in individual managers' ethical judgment and discretion. If decision making is decentralized while managers are still required to base their decisions on a rigid model of rule compliance, the net result is no different than if all decisions are made by one central authority. The goal is to provide ethical training and such assistance that at the local level, under pressure of time or away from oversight, managers and employees will be more likely to make the ethical decision than not.

A Child's Tale

Several years ago, Corning Glass Works found itself assailed in the press as an exploiter of child labor. It seems that a joint venture in India in which Corning had a minority interest was being supplied by a company that employed children in its factory. Although Corning did not have managerial control over the situation, Corning was being held accountable.

One Response

The simplest procedure would have been for Corning to deny any prior knowledge of the problem and to issue a statement expressing dismay and assuring the public that Corning in no way, directly or indirectly, supported the practice.

A Better Response

According to Van Campbell, then vice chairman of Corning Glass Works, "After we picked ourselves up and ascertained the facts, we asked ourselves what we could have done to prevent the damage and the scandal."

Management at Corning wondered whether the incident could have been avoided if there had been more candor and autonomy throughout the organization. They were particularly concerned that local managers in the corporation might have known what was going on but never bothered to tell the people who needed to know. No one paused for ethical reflection; no one assumed responsibility.

The Answer

It was concluded that such a lack of candor and autonomy, if pervasive, could be a source of future problems not only in Corning's international vendor relations, but also, and perhaps more ominously, it could have a devastating effect on quality control.

The Program

In response, Corning launched a successful Total Quality program. Its goal was to impress upon every employee the importance of individual responsibility and to put in place incentives and operational supports that encouraged candor, initiative, and autonomy. The manager who is on the spot would be encouraged to make a judgment as to whether others needed to be brought into the decision-making process. In the child labor case, the damage might have been prevented if this kind of individual discretion had been encouraged.

The answer to avoiding hazards in implementing ethical reporting vehicles is to develop a corporate commitment to autonomy. At the Norton Company, for example, there is an essential trust that no one will be embarrassed for taking an ethical stand even if it means temporary harm to the business. Says former corporate senior counsel Ronald Marcks, "This is not the kind of company where moral authority is handed down from on high. Every manager is responsible for being able to recognize and interpret an ethical problem. It should get decided at a manager's own level. On the other hand, if there is any question about it being handled properly, the question should be moved on."

Marcks was describing a corporate philosophy that integrates good intentions with a program likely to produce good results.

15

ETHICAL DECISION MAKING IS NOT INSTINCTIVE
TEACH, TEACH, TEACH

We now know that effective ethics initiatives do not rely just on written codes of compliance and telephone numbers. Employees cannot be expected to consult a manual or pick up a phone unless they first recognize the existence of an ethical dilemma.

If we are not looking for something, we may not see it, even if it is right in front of us. Without intention or a point of focus, there most likely is no awareness. Ethical problems can be like that. We need to don "moral glasses" if we are to see them; otherwise they might escape our attention. The level of ethical awareness of employees needs to be raised and cultivated. This is a matter of teaching—of bringing out what is really already there in their own ethical intuitions.

Today's employees are a diverse lot spanning a broad range of ages and experiences. Some have served in the military; others have never known the disciplines of family life. Some are freethinkers; some prefer rigid routines. Some come from cultures in which sharing personal information and gifts is a mark of friendship; others find such behavior intrusive and unwelcome.

Not all employees, therefore, will view situations in the same way and be able to identify an ethical conflict or spot a violation of company policy. It is only by comprehensive ethics training programs, workshops, and materials that employees will begin to "sing from the same hymn book" about ethics. This is not to say that there cannot be legitimate ethical disagreements; there can be and there are. But before such ethical debate can occur, employees must first learn to recognize the existence of an ethical issue in front of them that may or may not need clarification and discussion.

What Do You Want to Accomplish?

Before setting up a training program, think carefully about your objectives. Programs should be designed to meet specific goals, and not all goals may be achieved in a single session.

- Do you want to deepen the level of ethical awareness of the participants?

- Do you want to provide participants with decision-making tools?

Sandy, a new supervisor, is annoyed that she has been asked to visit the company's loading dock area during tonight's third shift as part of an audit assignment. When she arrives, she is angry because there is no one there to help her; the loading dock is deserted. The next morning, she checks the time cards and notes that the night supervisor signed out the loading dock crew at 4 AM, three hours *after* her visit. Will Sandy have the support structure to pursue the situation?

- Do you want participants to be able to recognize business ethics issues?

- Do you want participants to reflect on ethical issues and discuss them?

- Do you want participants to examine the values, policies, and goals of the company?

There are four developmental stages in ethics training. What stage do you expect your participants to reach?

1. Ethical awareness

2. Ethical reasoning

3. Ethical action

4. Ethical leadership

John is a buyer for Custom Tableworks, a manufacturing firm. Company policy clearly prohibits him from receiving gifts or favors of any kind from suppliers. He understands the policy but is puzzled. CT's sales representatives give valuable premiums, trips and favors to CT's customers. Should he question the accepted practice?

Who Is the Audience?

Training programs and training tools should be customized to fit the audience.

- Will the training be for executive-level employees only?

- Will the training be for rank-and-file employees?

- Will the training be for new employees or for those with seniority?

- Will the training be conducted department by department, or will it be cross-functional?

- Will the training be limited to a particular subject area?
- How long will a training session last?

Susan is a new sales representative. A single mother, she desperately needs her job at the *Breeze*, her town's daily newspaper. Her current assignment is to sell advertising for the
Breeze's special automotive section running the following
month. The specific sales goals she is to reach are listed on a
chart in the sales office. Susan, unfortunately, is having a difficult time generating ads because auto sales have been slow
and the local car dealers are cutting expenses. Her boss has
made it clear that he is displeased with her track record to
date. What can she do to ensure that she meets her goals and
keeps her job?

How Do Participants Learn?

Some employees learn best by reading; some cannot read at all.
Some learn visually and remember best what they see on a televi-
sion screen. Some respond best to verbal presentations; others
find these sleep-inducing. Some prefer to role play; others dread it.
Some like to discuss hypothetical cases; others find such discussions a boring waste of time and prefer to be given the answers
directly.

Design your program with care.

What Should Be Included?

Ethics training programs cannot be plucked off the shelf and
plugged into any corporation or organization. Each program
must be individually crafted according to the business issues of

> Cynthia has been asked by her company to attend a three-day
> conference related to new developments in her field. Her boss
> told her that the company would take care of all expenses for
> her trip, all she had to do was keep track of them. The confer-
> ence was held at an all-inclusive resort and the program
> allowed one afternoon of free time. Cynthia rented golf clubs
> and played a round of golf, for which she was charged $120.
> She is now filling out her expense report. Does the company
> have a clear policy? Was it communicated to her?

the industry and the company as well as the particular culture and
mission of the organization.

With that said, however, the most effective programs all contain these common elements:

- Opening remarks by a senior executive
- An introduction by the trainer
- A discussion of general ethical principles and business ethics
  in particular
- An overview of how companies and organizations are inte-
  grating ethical considerations into their operations
- A discussion of the framework and guidelines for business
  ethics decision making
- Response to various common questions, concerns and myths
  about business ethics
- Dramatization of ethical dilemmas
- Discussion of the dilemmas, including identification of the
  ethical issues, application of ethical principles and guide-

lines, and consideration of alternative plans of action

- Presentation of ethical dilemmas specifically designed for or occurring at the company or organization
- Discussion and resolution of each dilemma
- Design or critique of ethics initiatives at the company or organization, such as its code of ethics and its guidance system for reporting problems or seeking help

---

Beatrice was cleaning off her desk for the night when Martin, her boss, stopped by with a sheaf of papers in his hand and a furl on his brow. "Beatrice, I'm in a bind. I need this presentation revised for tomorrow's board meeting and I was hoping you could stay. The other problem is that we've been told we can't authorize any more overtime this month. I'll have to make it up to you in comp time or take care of it next month. Okay?"

What Stories Should We Choose?

All ethics training seminars should contain some real-life examples of ethical problems actually faced by employees. In choosing which anecdotes and cases to discuss, though, consider the factors that influence individuals in their ethical decision making. Some may be more applicable than others to your participants, and this should be a factor in your selection of stories:

- What do employees perceive to be the behavior of their supervisors?
- Are there formal policies already existing that impact upon ethical dilemmas?

- What is the ethical climate of the business or industry?
- What is the behavioral norm of the participants' peers in the company?
- What are the financial and other needs of the participants?
- What is the moral climate of the community or society in which the individuals or company are operating?

Do We Really Want to Teach Ethics?

Ethics is the study of what is good or right for human beings. Ethics is the study of the goals they ought to pursue and the actions they ought to perform.

Teaching ethics is not without risk. It is not necessarily keeping everyone in line and following orders; it may even be disruptive. Employees trained in ethical reasoning and ethical action may demonstrate their autonomy by exercising ethical leadership —and by challenging the conduct of others in the company, including superiors. Managers should recognize that this is not bad, but rather healthy, to the organization as well as to the individuals who comprise the organization.

SECTION FOUR

RUN IT LIKE A BUSINESS
... AN *ETHICAL* BUSINESS

16

UNITED WAY OF AMERICA
WHO'S MINDING THE STORE?

February 27, 1992—William Aramony, president of United Way of America, is forced to resign amidst allegations that, over a five-year period, he and two close aides transferred more than a million dollars a year to other organizations they controlled. It is also alleged that they spent hundreds of thousands in United Way funds on personal travel and on what some have called excessive pensions and insurance plans for themselves, some of which were approved by the board of directors. It is also charged that Aramony has carried on an affair with a minor and that United Way funds have been used to pay for her travel and expenses.

Following Aramony's resignation, Kenneth Dam, interim president of United Way of America, says: "These [allegations] are disturbing, and will certainly outrage people who have given their hard-earned money week by week to help the United Way help those in need. They will, and should, feel betrayed."

June 1995—Aramony is convicted on 25 felony counts including conspiracy, fraud, money-laundering and filing false tax returns. **His sentence**—7 years in a minimum-security prison.

In the Beginning ...

The United Way tale begins all the way back in 1887 in Denver, Colorado. Community leaders were looking for ways to meet the needs of pioneer families who were moving West. They decided to create a single charitable organization that would be able to raise funds, coordinate diverse support activities, and more efficiently deliver a wide variety of services. Out of their efforts, the United Way concept was born. Soon thereafter, civic leaders in other communities fashioned similar charitable organizations to meet local needs. Thus were born the Community Chest, Red Feather, and local United Way chapters. Though the names differed, they were all based on simple acts of charity, of people helping people.

In the 1960s, as public funding of health and social services increased, some donors questioned the future necessity of orga- nized voluntary charity. The national association of local United Ways formed a selection committee to find a national leader who would guide the organization through troubled times.

William Aramony, who had a masters degree in social work from Boston College, had worked during the 1960s for communi- ty service organizations around the country. He was well known among his peers as an innovative leader, and had gained attention for leading the United Way effort in Miami to record fund-raising results. At that time, the search committee was leaning toward choosing a well known person from outside the organization to lead it. Reportedly, Aramony objected and threatened to lead a boycott unless a United Way regional professional was selected.

His name was subsequently placed on the short list and, as part of the process, the search committee hired private investigators to look into his background. According to reports, the chairman of the board then confronted Aramony with "compromising information." Aramony's response was, "My private life is my own business." He then provided the board with assurances that apparently satisfied everyone, but the incident may have been a prelude of things to come. As John Glaser, a longtime Aramony colleague at the United Way, has since written, "Twenty-three years later, this attitude towards his personal lifestyle would help contribute to his downfall. It was also an attitude that one could say was 'pure Aramony.' "

In December 1970, Aramony was named the national executive of what was later to become the United Way of America. He brought to the job enthusiasm, charisma, tremendous leadership ability, and a deep-rooted commitment to the mission of the United Way. Above all else, he wanted to help people in need. The many changes he introduced at the United Way were intended to make it a more efficient organization that was better able to fulfill its mission. From the very beginning he encouraged local offices to become more like businesses. At the national level he moved headquarters to Alexandria, Va.; he was the driving force behind the establishment of a national service and training center; and he created the means for providing research, marketing, communications, government relations, and other support services to member United Way organizations across the country. Aramony was results-oriented and an entrepreneur. As new programs proliferated, the United Way not only survived, it thrived.

His character and success earned him the trust and respect of those who worked with him. Though some accused him of being arrogant, even his critics recognized his accomplishments and called him a "genius" in his field.

The "genius" of Aramony was his vision, and his legacy is the complete transformation of the way human service providers are funded in North America. He transformed the United Way of America from a collection of unaffiliated local foundations into an integrated network, often with local business leaders as chairs. Having recruited nationally known executives as his own board members, Aramony was able to complete the most important phase of transformation—that of the United Way of America into a presence in nearly every workplace.

Progressive strides also blossomed inside the organization, Operation Blueprint being the most notable. Designed to attract more minorities and women into volunteer and staff positions at the United Way, this program was initiated long before such diversity programs were generally accepted. In this initiative, Aramony was a pioneer. The new faces he brought in represented a breadth of experiences and background and were enthusiastic supporters of both United Way's mission and of Aramony.

Thanks in large measure to the changes brought about by Aramony, the United Way nationwide raises about $3 billion for more than 45,000 local charities in an average year. As our tale unfolds, it's important not to lose sight of the good works that Aramony did and which the United Way continues to do.

Given the commitment to doing good, the tremendous progress in the early years, and the lasting legacy, how do we explain what happened? How did the leader of United Way of America fall so far?

Run It Like a Business

The human service, nonprofit world has changed from its grass roots advocacy traditions to a more businesslike bottom line approach to delivery of services. Many volunteers started out in the advocacy world of issues, popular movements, and a mission-oriented commitment.

Bruce Hopkins, a legal expert on charitable organizations, explains the nature of the changes: "Today the management of nonprofit organizations is more sophisticated and aggressive than ever before. This is due in part to the pressures of demand for more services at a time when government funding for them is declining. Traditional ways of raising money are proving to be insufficient, forcing nonprofit organizations into more creative ways of generating financial support. They are becoming more 'efficient,' 'entrepreneurial,' and 'businesslike.'"

If managers of nonprofits are now running their organizations "more like businesses," it's important that they choose their business models wisely. Our earlier chapters presented numerous examples of before and after stories—of companies that faced moral and legal crises, learned tough lessons, and developed **the ethical edge.** Managers of nonprofits can also learn from these examples. They should run their operations "like a business," but more importantly they should run them "like an *ethical* business." The stakes may be even higher in the nonprofit world, where managers are relying on the generosity of the donor public and taxpayers to fund their services. Those who contribute to nonprofits generally do not receive services in return; they give to support services for others and out of a philanthropic sense of charity and responsibility. Nonprofits must work hard to earn the respect and trust of their supporters and cannot afford to alienate them.

Some managers in the nonprofit realm complain that the public is now demanding more businesslike efficiency from them, while at the same time holding the nonprofits to an unrealistic, high ethical standard based on nonprofits' traditional missions. These managers see this as an impossible dilemma. How, they ask, can they be efficient, businesslike *and* ethical?

What these managers fail to understand is that the public is holding not only nonprofits to a high ethical standard, but they have also made the same demand of for-profit organizations. For-profits have begun to respond to the call for efficiency and ethics; nonprofits, for the most part, have not. While the 1980s were a time of growth and plenty for many, it was also an era of gradually rising ethical expectations. Good times sometimes mask subtle change, so that when the ethical bar was raised, few at the United Way of America seemed to notice.

Is This Any Way to Handle an Investigation?

Allegations of wrongdoing by William Aramony first surfaced privately in 1990. All nine of the board's outside directors received an identical anonymous letter dated January 24, 1990. Aramony's board then was a "Who's Who" of corporate America including John Akers, then chairman of IBM; W.R. Howell, chairman of J.C. Penney; James Robinson, then chairman and CEO of American Express; and Edward Brennan who, at the time, was chairman both of Sears, Roebuck and of United Way. The letter they all received claimed that Aramony had been having affairs with two sisters, one of whom was a minor. The writer also said that Aramony had used United Way of America funds to hush up the affairs. Lending credibility to the letter was the fact that on the day it arrived, Aramony was traveling in London and Egypt with the sisters.

Brennan requested a meeting with Aramony as soon as he returned. Brennan has related, "I told him the United Way is a very fragile organization and that if there was any truth to these allegations, it could be damaging.... I said, 'Bill, these are very serious allegations. Be forthright.'"

Aramony denied everything and Brennan gave him the benefit of the doubt. Brennan reported the meeting to the other outside directors and, as he later said, "unwittingly misinformed" them that the letter's charges were unfounded. Digging a little deeper, Brennan questioned other senior executives at United Way and they also denied that there was any truth to the allegations. One of these executives was Lisle Carter, Jr., the United Way's general counsel. Carter, though, really did know more than he told Brennan. He later explained his silence with the statement: "I thought it was Mr. Aramony's place to make [matters] clear.... There was only one alternative for me. That was to try to work through Mr. Aramony with the situation or resign and tell the board. I did not follow that [second] course."

If Brennan or Carter thought at the time that the letter and "investigation" were sufficient to send a message to Aramony, they should have quickly realized that this was not going to happen. In April 1990, just two months after his talk with Brennan, Aramony and the younger sister were again off to London. For this trip the United Way reportedly paid $2,034 for lodging, $365 for meals, and $3,435 for her airfare.

A Betrayal of Trust

On February 16, 1992, two years after the anonymous letter, the first of two stories appeared in the *Washington Post* under a front page headline:

> PERKS, PRIVILEGES AND POWER IN A NONPROFIT WORLD
> **Head of United Way of America Praised, Criticized for
> Running It Like a Fortune 500 Company**

Other articles soon followed, including a nationally syndicated column by Jack Anderson and Michael Binstein titled: "Charity Begins at Home for United Way." The accusations focused on three categories:

- **Salary and Perks**—The articles listed Aramony's salary and benefits as $463,000 ($390,000 salary) and cited other expenses and perks: a rosewood table in his office; "chauffeured automobiles" costing $20,000 a year; $40,700 on transatlantic trips aboard the supersonic *Concorde,* and $92,265 in frequent trips for himself, his wife, or other companions to vacation meccas and to Worcester, Mass., Gainesville, Fla., and other cities where Aramony's family lived. In most cases, according to reports, no United Way business was conducted on these trips.

- **Nepotism and Cronyism**—The first *Post* article was critical of the hiring of Thomas Merlo, a longtime Aramony friend, to be the organization's chief financial officer. Aramony was quoted as saying, "I didn't [check his background] because I knew him." Merlo received a salary of $211,000 plus an apartment and weekly travel expenses to and from his Florida home. The article also criticized the hiring of Aramony's son

Robert to be the president of Sales Service/ America, a spin-off organization that was created following a board-authorized study. It sold United Way of America products and grossed $6 million per year. The job was reportedly never advertised, and no one else was interviewed for it.

- Spin-offs—United Way of America provided more than $900,000 seed money to create Partnership Umbrella, Inc., a spin-off organization to provide discount services to charities. Very successful at first, it ran into trouble when it began buying real estate and bailing out other spin-offs. Among its purchases were more than $1.3 million in real estate in New York City, Florida, and Alexandria, Va. This sum included $434,000 for a condominium in New York City for Aramony so he wouldn't need to pay for hotel rooms. Partnership Umbrella, Inc., was run by one of Aramony's longtime friends, Stephen Paulachak, who had served previously as United Way's chief financial officer.

Not surprisingly, the allegations of Aramony's affair again came to light. Aramony had apparently met a woman on a plane in 1986, hired her to work at United Way, and carried on an affair with her. After she clashed with him, Stephen Paulachak offered her another United Way job if she would keep quiet. Aramony then turned his attention to her younger sister, giving her money to construct a sun room at her house in Gainesville, money to pay her income tax, and "consulting payments," even though she did no work. When the details of the relationship became public, John Akers, then the United Way chairman, confronted Aramony.

Aramony tried to persuade him to ignore the charges since they had been "checked out by Ed Brennan."

Who's Minding the Store?

Aramony, like many presidents, ran his organization with a free hand. Results were excellent and the board was pleased. Final authority for the United Way of America, however, did ultimately rest with the board of directors, who approved Aramony's contract and compensation, and who were also responsible for his actions.

When the crisis came to light, board members were never charged with any wrongdoing, but critics have contended that they were too easily duped. Larry D. Horner, retired chairman of the board of KPMG Peat Marwick and head of the Audit Committee of the United Way board at the time, admitted that the board should have been "a little more quizzical." Another board member, Ragan Henry, a partner in a Philadelphia law firm, added, "Certainly I have learned a lesson: I'm not going to take things at face value." In a later effort to explain his thinking at the time, he said, "When you deal with a trusted executive who's been around a long time, there is a tendency to take a lot of things that he says at face value, and not delve into and look around a lot."

In his defense, Aramony claimed that the board was made aware of all financial matters and that they reviewed and regularly approved financial reports. It's one thing if the board approved these matters after a full investigation and careful oversight; it's quite another matter, however, if the board relied exclusively on Aramony and other senior officials to distill the facts for them, and then, after a few questions, rubber-stamped his proposals. Consider a typical board meeting.

United Way of America board members would receive an inch-thick booklet a week or two before a meeting. This contained favorable press clippings, financial statements, upbeat committee reports, and an agenda. The agenda was structured to direct the flow of discussion toward program goals rather than operational ones. The single functioning internal committee, the Audit Committee, had but one role: to approve the hiring of the outside auditing firm and review its reports.

Some have questioned whether the meetings were rigorous enough. They point, for example, to a report that a mere 20 minutes of one meeting was given over to discussing the organization's spending and management. The rest of the meeting consisted of rosy reviews of committee activities. The 20 minutes were hardly enough time to delve into any serious issues. It is doubtful that during those 20 minutes anyone asked about the $2.1 million loan that Aramony had approved, one month prior to the meeting, for Sales Service/America, the spin-off headed by his son.

Some board members who had an advocacy rather than a business background were quickly in over their heads when the agenda turned to financial matters. "As adults you hate to appear stupid. So you act like you pretend to know financial reports, and you don't ask questions if the auditors tell you everything is fine," one has suggested. Another board member noted that probing questions by board members of nonprofits are too often thought of as bad manners. "If I liked him [Aramony] less I might have been more demanding and in search of the negative. Liking others and wanting to be liked are human qualities, but not a luxury we can afford. How do we guard against it?"

The scandal at United Way of America had far-reaching implications, despite the fact that the organization Aramony ran had more in common with a $30 million national trade association than a charity. Its purpose was to serve as an umbrella organization for its member United Ways, which raised money locally and redistributed it to social service agencies.

Unfortunately, this distinction may have been lost on the public, which was outraged by the wide disparity between Aramony's lifestyle and compensation, and the pressing needs of the disadvantaged whom local United Way volunteers were assisting. Local United Way chapters withheld their dues to United Way of America, and individual donors across the country withheld or decreased their contributions as well. While United Way leaders scrambled to explain that the scandal at national headquarters did not reflect how local organizations were run, they were also furious that the public attention given to the Aramony case confused local contributors and diverted attention from their mission: to help those in need. The entire episode was, as a preliminary audit characterized it, "a story of excess and of values lost."

"Not Yet a Change of Soul"

In the wake of the turmoil, United Way of America has taken significant steps in the right direction toward an ethical culture. Under its new president, Elaine Chao, it has added eight new members to the board and taken steps to ensure that a diversity of views are present, including those of representatives from local

chapters. It has created six new board committees with responsibility for areas such as budget and finance. It has written and distributed a code of ethics, and it has tightened up internal financial
controls throughout the organization.

The changes at the board level were certainly needed, especially because in some ways being a nonprofit director is more
challenging than being a for-profit director.

- Too often, busy and perhaps overcommitted nonprofit directors view service on a board as an honorary post, or a way of
  making a contribution to the community rather than as a
  position requiring a great deal of time and effort, and which
  may incur potential "reputational liability." They are willing
  to donate wealth and wisdom, but only if it does not take too
  much time. These same individuals may sit as directors of
  public companies or mutual funds; because on such boards
  they are compensated and have extensive legal liability, they
  may be diligent board members.

- For the reason that their organizations are private and unregulated, nonprofit directors may have fewer resources to help
  them ascertain the truth of information presented to them.
  In addition, if there is not a high level of candor in the organization or at the board, they are likely to have fewer internal
  sources of information.

- In the nonprofit world it is more difficult to reach consensus
  about clear, objective measures of financial success, in contrast to those in the for-profit world. For-profit directors can
  always begin by looking at profitability, market share, and
  stock price. Discrepancies or questions in these areas can

often lead to further questions that may turn up wrongdoing, irregularities, or lax internal controls. No comparable starting points exist for nonprofit directors, particularly if the human service mission of the organization, its tradition, or its precedents become the overriding focus of attention, rather than its financial reports.

- Nonprofit directors and administrators often assume that because those involved in the organization have a commitment to its charitable mission, they therefore deserve a higher degree of trust. This can lead to complacency and a feeling that oversight and controls are less urgently needed.

- Nonprofits are often run and staffed by volunteers as well as paid staff, and they experience frequent turnover. In a continually changing organization, too much power and authority can be concentrated in the hands of the few who remain over time.

Can another scandal occur at United Way of America? Businesswoman Cheryle Wills, former United Way chairperson of the board in Cleveland, director of United Way International, and a member of the recent United Way of America presidential search committee, recently cautioned that the changes to date may not go far enough. A deeper and abiding shift in moral standards is needed to protect against complacency that can arise in any organization: "I think we have to put a stake in the sand. If things get better, we may go back to the same old ways," she has said. "We need to put in place a values system that survives. We may have had a change of perception, but not yet a change of soul."

17

TEXAS A&M UNIVERSITY
A LESSON IN "INSTITUTIONAL ARROGANCE"

In August 1994, Dr. Barry Thompson gave his first address as the new chancellor of Texas A&M, the nation's third-largest university system. The university was going through the worst year anyone could remember. Indicative of the turmoil was the fact that Thompson was the third person to be named A&M chancellor within that short stretch of time. Olive Talley, a controversial, award-winning reporter for the *Dallas Morning News,* summed up the mood of those present:

"Aggies proclaim themselves a breed apart, a university-based community whose bonds are stronger than outsiders can understand. They have long spoken of their honor code, which extols the highest ideals, and of their fighting spirit, best exemplified by the school's revered football team.

But for many Aggies today, the fight is against demoralization. Or it's a battle against the feeling that their traditions have been betrayed. Or it's a struggle just to know whom to be angry at."

A Texas state representative, who is also an Aggie alum, had a clearer idea of what was to blame: "It's been a failure of leadership on the part of the board of regents that has set these things in motion.... And it's still not clear who the good guys and the bad guys are on this."

Against this backdrop of confusion, anger, Aggie pride and frustration, Dr. Thompson reminded his audience that: "Education is about values. Education is about civility, about literature, the arts. It's about the highest expression mankind can make... the charge we have from the people of Texas is to do good things for good folks."

He called on the employees to stop internal turf battles, start taking risks, and start taking action: "I'm tired of strategic planning as an end in itself.... I challenge you to do some strategic doing." Then showing refreshing candor, he added: "I do not have all the answers, but I'm absolutely excited about the few I do have." With that he announced Operation Lone Star, a plan for reaffirming the mission of the university and for resolving its internal problems. He hoped that this program would be the start of an effort to recapture Texas A&M's credibility with the public. He knew that something had to be done. After all, during the previous 11 months the university had been investigated by the Texas Rangers and the FBI; a grand jury had issued indictments, and damning internal audits had been released. Everyone was trying to get to the bottom of one scandal or another. Stories and rumors rocked the campus and repercussions were felt across the state of Texas. Which of the stories were true? Were they the product of vindictive journalists or ambitious prosecutors and investigators? Or were they signs of an institution that was out of control and over the ethical edge? What were the problems that had brought them to this juncture?

"The Philadelphia Project"

Reports were published that a chemistry professor, Dr. John O'M. Bockris was conducting fanciful research called "The Philadelphia Project," which purported to turn mercury into gold. The professor, though a bit eccentric, never intended to defraud anyone. In fact, far from being a "mad scientist," he is considered by many to be the "father of electro-magnetic chemistry" and his research was really a series of experiments to find a cost-effective way of effecting the "transmutation of metals." A blue ribbon panel at A&M exonerated him of scientific fraud and there continues to be criticism that the published stories unfairly represented his work. In the end, however, the incident did embarrass the university. In two previous projects it was reported that the professor "made public announcements boasting of his scientific discoveries…causing embarrassment to the University." Nevertheless, no one at the university did anything to control Dr. Bockris, his colleagues, or his backers.

The professor allegedly did not comply with research protocols nor was he in compliance with university financial procedures. In fact he was accused of circumventing "normal procedures," of not reimbursing the university for overhead, and avoiding internal oversight. His defenders, however, point out that a major part of the problem was that "normal procedures" were not clear. The policy on "gifts and grants" was ambiguous. The lack of such controls cost the university somewhere between $20,000 and $90,000. And, to make matters worse, the project was started with $200,000 in seed money raised by William Telander using the A&M name. Telander was subsequently convicted of securities fraud.

"Give My Regards..."

Texas A&M Vice President of Finance and Administration Robert Smith was convicted of soliciting trips from a vendor for himself, his wife and others. In his 23 years at the university, Smith had worked his way up from auditor to chief financial officer and was A&M's third-highest ranking administrator.

Barnes & Noble, the national bookstore chain, was negotiating with Smith for a $23 million contract with the university to run its bookstores. Smith was convicted of soliciting trips from Barnes & Noble while the company was negotiating for the contract. In all, the cost of the trips totaled $37,000. Those joining Smith on the trips were his wife, the chair of the board of regents Ross Margraves, and Margraves' wife. Prosecutors detailed four such New York trips of the Smith-Margraves party. Expenses included $12,000 for first-class airfare, $230-a-night rooms at the Waldorf-Astoria and the Helmsley Palace, theater tickets to *The Goodbye Girl*, three meals that alone cost $2,200, and four-day limousine charges of $1,804. In addition, it was reported that Smith hosted Barnes & Noble executives and their wives in Texas for weekend football games and meals at a cost to the university of $4,000.

Barnes & Noble was eventually awarded the contract even though there were allegations that its bid was $369,000 higher than that of its chief competitor, Follett College Stores, Inc.

At her husband's trial, Pat Smith defended her travel expenses, rationalizing that she was an "ambassador for A&M." She told the jury that at the end of one of their trips, "we were all hugging...because it had been a good trip" and bookstore executives told her: "We're looking forward to having ya'll come back."

Robert Smith denied any wrongdoing, arguing that all the expenses were allowable and besides, he said, A&M benefited because it didn't have to pick up the tab.

Though the Smiths characterized their trip as routine business, some of the bookstore executives told a different story. According to their testimony, not only was no business conducted during the most expensive of the New York weekend trips, but also Smith was only the second client of more than 100 Barnes & Noble college accounts that had asked to bring his spouse along. The prosecutor noted that Barnes & Noble could have said no and that its executives did agree to host the weekend trips. But, he added, "What do you expect someone facing a [multi-]million-dollar deal to say?" In his view the case was simple. "This is about when people are auctioning off parts of government for taxpayers, they should not personally benefit."

To this day there are many who believe this case should never have been prosecuted. They argue that this was a simple misunderstanding and that no one was trying to take advantage of the situation for personal gain. The Smiths legitimately believed that they were acting appropriately and were doing a service to the university. Critics see the case as an example of excessive litigation that turned a gesture of common courtesy into a criminal offense.

"Cups & Beverages"

In September 1993, an anonymous letter circulated throughout the state, accusing several high-ranking university officials of using their office for personal gain. As a result of the accusations, the Texas Rangers and the FBI began to investigate. A grand jury was convened and ten indictments were handed down. Texas A&M's

athletic director, the manager of business and facilities operations, a professor of oceanography, a professor of management, the vice president of student affairs, the executive secretary for the board of regents, and other administrators were charged with "tampering with government records." But what did they really do?

Over a period of years, members of the board of regents and other officials bought beer and wine at a local liquor store for their meetings and other official occasions. One year's bill for the regents totaled about $5,000. It was reported that the store submitted itemized bills listing the amounts and types of alcoholic beverages purchased.

When vouchers were submitted to the university's controller, however, the original invoices were replaced by hand-written invoices that were not from the liquor store but from a catering firm. The vouchers showed the same dates and amounts as the originals, but they listed the items as "food, soft drinks, ice and cups." The story became known around campus as the "cups & beverages" incident.

Most thought the matter was blown completely out of proportion. They argued that this was perhaps a technical violation, that no one intended to defraud or conceal anything, that it was a long-standing policy and employees were simply trying to comply. According to one report, one of the indictments was for reimbursement of less than five dollars for a bottle of cooking sherry. No one could remember how the policy had actually begun, but sometime in the 1960s the fiscal office refused to process vouchers for alcohol, even though it was perfectly legal to use state money for such purposes. However the policy began, though, employees knew that if they didn't comply, they wouldn't get reimbursed.

Others smelled blood. They felt that this was just the tip of the iceberg and that lax controls, perks, and arrogance were widespread. The severest critics of the university notwithstanding, almost everyone felt the secretaries and mid-level administrators who were indicted were scapegoats and the real blame should have been directed higher up. For those who felt this way, there was some consolation in announcements that the investigations by the Texas Rangers and the FBI were not yet completed; the investigators were hot on the trail of reports of "excessive spending" by the regents.

"Texas Is Big"

Between the years of 1991 and 1993 published reports alleged that the nine-member board of regents had spent more than $1.6 million for its own expenses. The reports claimed that during the previous four fiscal years $907,000—billed at $500 per hour—was spent to fly them throughout Texas on state-owned aircraft. Other notable expenses included $9,811 for floral arrangements for board meetings, a $144 bar bill for three regents in Las Vegas, $495 for food and drinks at one football game in California, $1,900 to repair two teapots and a candelabra, and $32,000 for air travel by spouses, children, and guests of the regents.

Former Governor Ann Richards appointed all nine regents who, according to published documents, contributed $190,500 to her campaign. The free-spending ways of the regents were impressive: They outspent their colleagues at the larger University of Texas System by $300,000 over three years, and they outspent all of the regents combined at the University of Houston, Texas Tech University, and the University of North Texas.

The regents defended their expenditures by noting that Texas is a big state and they cited the importance of attending events throughout the state and the difficulty of getting commercial flights. Watchdog groups and state legislators, however, saw things differently. One state senator noted that the method for financing regents' expenditures was "Byzantine" and he alleged that it was purposely designed to obscure accountability.

The "Runaway Freight Train"

Controversy erupted over plans to build a $120 million utility plant for A&M, which many thought was unnecessary. The project, described by university officials as a "runaway freight train," was eventually derailed—but not before the university spent $15 million and Tenneco Power Generation Company invested $60 million in the project. Was this just a bad business decision or did a lack of oversight at the highest levels allow a few to keep the plan rolling along months after it should have been stopped?

"Food Fight!"

Allegations of mismanagement and "plantation" working conditions in the university's food services department surfaced in an audit of its operations. According to some former employees, top university officials, including Robert Smith, blocked needed changes, while at the same time attempting to bring private contractors into the department. University officials then allegedly fired managers who opposed the privatization plan and later, in a particularly offensive strategy, criticized the fired managers for not making the changes that the managers had actually called for!

Operation Lone Star

The early 90s were not good years at Texas A&M. Clearly, by

1994 change was needed. So, almost immediately after assuming their new positions, Chancellor Thompson and Dr. Ray Bowen, president of the university, announced the first steps under Operation Lone Star. They tightened policies and controls to ensure that the problems of the past did not repeat themselves. Thompson also announced a series of meetings to be held across Texas, which, he hoped, would help build public trust. The meetings, however, were not designed to discuss the recent allegations of wrongdoing, or to discuss possible steps that could be taken to renew the ethical culture at Texas A&M. Instead, these meetings were designed, in the chancellor's frank words, to "influence the political process to get a larger piece of the pie." Critics noted that the effort was pragmatically necessary, but they feared it would be misunderstood. Thompson and Bowen were setting themselves up to be criticized for not focusing on renewing the university's traditional commitment to values and integrity.

Operation Lone Star's next initiative also seemed to be off the "ethics mark." The Texas A&M's regents unanimously approved two ethics guidelines, one for the board and one for employees. Unfortunately, in announcing the guidelines, the board of regents chair, Mary Nan West, could not conceal her lack of enthusiasm for the project. More importantly, she lost an opportunity at the same time to clearly establish her leadership in this area. She said that although she wasn't thrilled about having to adopt official ethics guidelines, she did so because "I guess we've been shot at so much, we decided we'd get our policy in black and white." And, she concluded, "I just feel that everybody knows the difference between right and wrong, and if they don't, they should, and it should not have to be written."

A few months later, in January of 1995, the state of Texas gave the university a "wake-up call" in the form of a tough audit. This was the first time the state had ever conducted a management audit of the university. The auditors found that management controls were broken and sometimes ignored, and that this contributed to "poor decision making, ineffective use of resources, weak oversight of operations, and a general lack of accountability."

The auditors praised the new leadership for the steps it had already taken to tighten up controls. And, to their credit, Thompson and Bowen not only accepted the findings but they acknowledged that it was a "good summation." Furthermore, they admitted that the problems were rooted in "institutional arrogance" by A&M's leadership. Dr. Bowen added, in a moment of candor and introspection: "We perceived ourselves to be unconstrained by rules and regulations."

Two weeks later, the board of regents met to respond to the state audit. The board's chair, Mary Nan West, agreed with Thompson and Bowen and did not dispute or criticize the auditor's report. Other board members, however, challenged the conclusions. West concluded the meeting by saying she would, "do what I can do" to "provide the leadership needed to ensure that the appropriate management controls, policies, and procedures are established and followed, and that officials and staff at all levels are held accountable for their actions."

But, as a final comment, she added, "One of the problems we've got is that no one's responsible for their actions."

Stay tuned. The ethical recovery at Texas A&M may not be over.

18

THE BUCK STOPS HERE
INSTITUTIONAL ETHICS
AND BOARDS OF TRUSTEES

We now know that ethical oversight stops at the board of trustee level. It is there that responsibility resides for ensuring the integrity and stability of a nonprofit institution. Trustees oversee policy and controls while delegating matters of leadership and management to the president or executive director of the institution and its senior staff; but, as recent scandals have revealed, it is often the president or executive director who leads and manages the board of trustees. A recipe for ethical crises? The ingredients are infrequent meetings, inadequate information flow, and procedures that turn trustees into rubber stamps, in combination with longevity in the corner office and frequent turnover or complacency in the boardroom.

But public scandals have one silver lining. They often grab the attention of trustees who suddenly find themselves spotlighted on the front pages of the local newspaper or called on the carpet by donors, constituents, and regulators. Often, only then do they realize they must do more than just delegate. They must

direct and inspire senior administrators to join them in a leadership role, developing a climate in which all individuals in the institution can act as leaders in their own sphere.

This emphasis on institutionwide responsibility comple-
ments structural changes occurring in many organizations. In the
business world, command-and-control pyramids have given way
to less hierarchy and flatter structures; decision making has been
pushed to the lowest possible level, requiring employees to rely on
their own instincts and abilities. The job of institutional leaders,
consequently, is to develop competence, integrity, reliability, and
vision in their employees.

The setup in nonprofit institutions is not that much different.
Leadership authority Warren Bennis asserts that managers do
things right; leaders do the right thing. Ultimately, the leadership
buck stops with the board of trustees, which must frame and oversee an ethical culture in which all members of the institution operate and which also provides all constituencies of the institution a
common and high standard of moral behavior.

Ethics Starts at the Top

It would seem obvious that the best ethical practice model starts
with a board of trustees that is itself ethical. Regrettably, many
boards neglect this self-examination.

- **Board composition** is the first matter. Ideally, trustees should
  be selected by a committee composed primarily or exclusively of trustees. In choosing those who would sit on the nominating committee, trustees should eliminate those individuals with possible conflicts of interest or undue influence.
  Those who fall in this category would be major suppliers,

outside counsel or accounting firms, persons whose only credential is a friendship with the president and even individuals who are major donors.

Nominating committees should give careful consideration to the criteria for choosing a trustee. Boards need not resemble Noah's ark, with each trustee representing a particular constituency. Every trustee has a responsibility to serve the institution as a whole and to be knowledgeable about all issues before the board. There is clear value, however, in bringing together diversity of life, of broad academic, professional, government and business experience, and their distinct qualifications and viewpoints.

Perhaps more important than title, status, or position is the candidate's reputation for personal integrity. Because it is difficult to evaluate a value system by reviewing a resume, nominating committees should strive to find out how candidates have demonstrated their particular ethical values throughout their careers and personal lives. Board candidates should present no conflict of interest issues, including holding positions on other competing boards or as executives of major suppliers, or other organizations having a major business relationship with the institution.

Assessing conflict of interest also involves analyzing the time demands placed on trustees. An overcommitted trustee may not be the best overseer of the institution, and periodic replacement of the individual by staff or "assistant to" representatives may not be what the nominating committee had in mind.

- **A structure that promotes maximum ethical effectiveness** is the next concern. A volunteer trustee, rather than the president or executive director, should chair the board and control the agenda. But it does not matter who chairs the board if the flow of information to trustees is limited. Harold Geneen, the former CEO of ITT Corporation, suggests that corporate boards are often ineffective because their opinions are based on what they are told by the institution's management.

The same danger may lie in nonprofit institutions where, because of the volunteer status of trustees, attention may be even more lax. Obviously it is not desirable to have trustees go behind the president's back to obtain important information, but it is critical to develop an open culture in which the president and others are encouraged and expected to inform the board of mistakes or problems in a timely manner. Trustees should work with the president to develop the type, frequency, and amount of information needed for meeting preparation, and this should be sent to members well in advance of the meeting. Trustees also should scrutinize the number, frequency, agenda, and makeup of board committees to guard against conflicts and to ensure the oversight of institutional controls. Audit and other committees that oversee financial controls should meet and report to the full board more frequently than other committees; trustees should rotate service on committees; and term limits on committees may be desirable.

● Finally, the board's ongoing operation should be conducted in an ethical manner to maximize effectiveness. Diligent boards conduct an annual performance evaluation of the president; only a few trustees are conducting self-initiated and peer evaluations of the board's own effectiveness and that of its members, however. It is obviously not easy for trustees to ask for the resignation of a fellow trustee, but they might find a model in corporate guidelines, such as those from General Motors, suggesting that trustees should volunteer to resign if significant job responsibilities change. Trustees should also volunteer to resign if nonattendance at meetings, increased job responsibilities or other factors limit their continued effectiveness as board members. In the absence of such voluntary resignation, the chairman must step forward and ask for appropriate action.

Red Flags

There is no short, quick list of the red flags that may alert diligent trustees to potential ethical problems. The following have all surfaced publicly, though, and can serve as a cautionary road map for boards:

1. **Conflicts of interest.** Are policies in place that prohibit or require disclosure of potential conflicts related to transactions with outside vendors or among departments, trustees, or employees? Some institutions require consulting assignments over a modest dollar limit to be approved by the board.

2. **Employee, donor, recipient or client complaints.** Is important information about complaints reaching the trustee level?

Such information may reveal problems before they get out of hand and can also help give trustees a clearer understanding of the institution's culture. This, in turn, can aid trustees in developing a moral environment for all constituencies, as well as preventing future ethical lapses.

3. **Improper use of institutional or endowment assets.** Are trustees aware of the use of assets, and are there policies and procedures in place to reveal any abuse?

4. **Ongoing practices or allegations regarding invasion of privacy or misuse of confidential information.** The increased use of communications technology, such as e-mail and voice mail as well as telecommuting capabilities, requires up-to-date policies about privacy and use of proprietary information. Conflicts between dissemination of information and its confidential or proprietary nature are more likely to occur in health care organizations, academic institutions, and human service providers.

5. **Pressures on revenue streams or balance sheets.** It is often easier for individuals to act ethically in good economic times than in bad, though even in good economic times employees and volunteers may experience undue pressure to cut corners. Questionable tactics eventually hurt the institutional integrity of the organization.

6. **Insensitivity in downsizing or restructuring.** Even nonprofits are not immune from downsizing. There are legitimate business reasons to reduce operations, eliminate staff, close facilities or merge with other institutions, as well as change the way the organization operates. Such activities have ethical,

financial, legal and operational repercussions, but perhaps none are as difficult to deal with as the consequences involving volunteers, staff, and recipients.

7. **Unjustifiable compensation and benefits.** Perhaps no issue is as troublesome for trustees to resolve as the appropriate level and structure of compensation and benefits for senior staff. Trustees must balance the organization's interest in attracting and retaining talent with the goals of achieving fairness and reasonableness, particularly in the nonprofit sector and in the eyes of donors and the public.

8. **Lack of full disclosure.** Institutions are less likely to face ethical crises if trustees insist on a culture of full disclosure to all constituencies. Whether the issue is the institution's investment policies, the salary of its president, expenses and perks for officers, or the waiver of fees to a certain group of service recipients, the ethical course of conduct is generally to be forthright and honest.

9. **Events that damage institutional image and reputation.** Whether it is allegations of sexual harassment, unsafe working conditions or practices, unfair employment policies, environmental issues or lack of internal controls, an ethical lapse impacts the ongoing reputation of the institution. How trustees deal with such events when they arise often determines how long-lasting the damage will be.

10. **Amoral institutional culture.** Incidents of racism, expense abuses, waiver of standards or procedures, or other ethical lapses often occur because everyone, including the trustees, is operating on the same wavelength: "This is a white school";

"We don't get paid enough in the nonprofit world so we deserve this"; "We'll accept this student because we need a winning basketball team this year." These are simple examples of overriding cultural mores that are understood by all. Diligent trustees should ask what the cultural mores are at their institution and whether they meet the standard of "the ethical point of view."

In Summary

Trustees, directors, fiduciaries, and others are not less ethical than anyone else. Too often, unfortunately, they have given little or no thought to developing a moral institutional culture within which individuals can act ethically. Causes of unethical actions are quite often systemic and not simply the result of isolated incidents. Trustees should examine themselves to see if their institutional structures and relations are compatible with ethical behavior. If they are not, then it is the business of the board to do the right thing and provide the ethical leadership for all.

19

Appraise the Directors

We now know that directors should undergo performance appraisals just like everyone else in the organization. But if the buck truly stops with the board, who will do the appraisal?

Actually, anyone can. A motivated board should do its own self-assessment, but a corporate officer, ethics officer, or even a shareholder or potential charitable donor is free to express opinions about the oversight of the board. (In cases of scandal, individual state attorneys general have themselves investigated boards and expressed distinct opinions about their oversight and diligence.)

In the corporate world, attention is squarely on directors. "Cosseted," "asleep at the switch," and "cronyism" are descriptions the financial press has used to describe some of them.

In truth, the situation is not much better in the nonprofit world, where some directors and trustees are no more lively than the "parsley on the fish" at a quarterly board luncheon. While the stakes may be lower than in the for-profit world, these directors often comprise a Who's Who of the business and civic community, and their own reputation is on the line if there is an abuse of public trust or a misuse of donor or taxpayer money. Just ask any

of the heavyweight directors of the New Era Partnership, allegedly a Ponzi-scheme memorable because of the status of its victims.

Thanks to scandals at United Way, Texas A&M, the NAACP,
the Freedom Forum, New Era Partnership, and other institutions,
changes are taking place in the nonprofit boardroom that mirror
the rapidly changing status of corporate governance in the business world. Directors and trustees are devoting more time and
attention to their duties and acting in an independent fashion.
The diligent ones are asking the following questions:

1. Do we have an up-to-date set of bylaws and do all trustees
    understand them?

2. Do all trustees understand their duties?

3. Does the chairman of the board understand his or her duties,
    and is the chairman independent from the president or exec-
    utive director?

4. Is our board the right size to be effective?

5. Does our board have fresh blood, or have some of us stayed
    too long and become stale?

6. Do we keep accurate minutes and follow up on open action
    points?

7. Do our members bring a breadth and diversity of business
    and life experience to the board?

8. Are all members diligent with respect to their duties?

9. Do all trustees receive materials for the meetings well in
    advance and have they read the materials before the meetings?

10. Do trustees periodically meet in executive session?

11. Do we completely understand the importance of a reputa-
    tion for integrity for each member of the board?

12. Do we have an independent selection process for new trustees?

13. Do we have a complete orientation program for new trustees and encourage them to ask questions and suggest new ways of doing things?

14. Do all members regularly attend board meetings and committee meetings?

15. Do we provide continuing education for trustees? Are we aware of the "best practice model" for trustee oversight?

16. Does every trustee participate vigorously and do all voices have equal weight?

17. Does our board have appropriate committees?

18. Do all trustees understand the mission, history and culture of the institution?

19. Do all trustees understand the finances of the institution?

20. Do all trustees understand the critical issues of the institution?

21. Do all trustees understand their legal duties, standards and responsibilities, including the regulatory authority that oversees the institution?

22. Do all trustees understand the public policy initiatives that impact upon this institution?

23. Does this board set goals for itself, for the institution, and its officers?

24. Does the board measure and review the goals?

25. Does the board act as a team?

26. Does the board effectively evaluate the president or executive director and senior officers?

27. Does the board conduct its own self-evaluation?

28. Does the board confront, deal with and solve sensitive problems?

29. Does the board have its own ethics committee that serves as an advocate of the ethical point of view in all board business?

30. Is the board taking steps to ensure that ethics will not be compartmentalized at the board level?

KEEPING THE ETHICAL EDGE

Business ethics is no longer an oxymoron, fad, or personal matter. It's finally an essential part of the mission for many companies, and it's working.

There's little need to explain why a solid ethical foundation is an important strategic tool. Just ask the former CEO of Bath Iron Works or the creditors of bankrupt Dow Corning, or the United Way donors and campaign volunteers across the country. These companies and individuals have learned that to ignore ethics is to run a very high risk, both in human and in financial terms.

There is abundant objective evidence that many companies and organizations are indeed taking ethics seriously. A 1990 survey conducted by the Center for Business Ethics revealed that 96 percent of the responding companies have now incorporated a written code of ethics, 43 percent conduct ethics workshops or training seminars, and 33 percent have instituted an ethics committee. Despite these impressive statistics, we know that ethics initiatives like these are just the first steps toward building an ethical organization.

They will not necessarily prevent ethical crises, as the tales of

BIW and Dow Corning demonstrate. What counts is what happens when crises do arise, and how those on the scene debate and resolve the conflicting ethical dilemmas.

Some of this ethical groundwork can be laid in advance. Today, forward-thinking business executives not only engage in continuous long-range planning around core business issues, but they also try to anticipate from whence might come the next moral crisis that could fell a company as quickly as a competitor's new product. We can suggest several challenges that lie ahead:

- Work is now considered an activity and not a place where employees go. Without a common gathering area such as a water cooler or cafeteria, it is difficult for institutions to develop a common culture and understanding of its values. In the virtual organization of tomorrow, an employee may not even know what a coworker is doing, or even who his or her coworkers are. Applying uniform ethical standards across organizations will be a communications challenge.

- Workers will continue to hold themselves aloof from corporate governance, motivated not by corporate loyalty but by the level of respect and autonomy the company places in them. These employees will demand a high degree of freedom, knowledge and responsibility. Institutions that remain rooted in a control-oriented, bureaucratic structure and which attempt to deliver ethics programs in such a manner will fail. The challenge for such organizations will be to let go from the top down.

- Individuals may be less able to check their private lives at the office door, so that deciding the point at which a company or coworker may intervene in behavior that does not affect job performance will be sensitive. Such concerns as domestic violence, failure to file taxes, use of alcohol or tobacco, or gambling outside of work may become issues of company concern in an era in which employees at all times are expected to adhere to commonly accepted moral standards.

- Performance appraisals will become more qualitative and less quantitative, and character will count as much as accomplishments. As Shirley Peterson, Northrop Grumman corporate vice president of ethics and business conduct, says, "Behavior that reflects trustworthiness, respect, responsibility, justice, fairness, caring, and citizenship will be prerequisites for membership on business teams in the knowledge era." Instilling and encouraging the attributes that make a person honorable—that comprise character—will become a major part of human resource training and evaluation programs.

- As the business world becomes connected by its own computer networks and the global Internet, the definition of privacy will change. "Confidentiality" may be a thing of the past and the lines may blur between what equipment, time, information, and supplies belong to the company and what belong to an individual.

- New technology will continue to create issues that were unheard of even a few years ago, a continuation of the challenges that technological advances have always presented. For example, if companies can develop sophisticated medical tests that uncover genetic defects, should individuals or their insurance companies be told the results? Companies are struggling over whether they should spend money on research and development of new techniques before they have resolved the enormously ethical implications of their use.

- Self-regulation will continue to be a formidable task for all types of industries, as a competing mix of public scandals and a resistance to government regulation forces ethical responsibility onto the opinion leaders of industry groups. Just as the Group of Thirty produced its study of global derivatives in 1993, recommending measures for managing risk (and which, if followed, would have prevented such events as the Baring PLC collapse), the onus for setting the ethical standards of commerce will rest with those who lead the very industries most needing supervision and guidance.

- The American business ethical culture is not the universal standard for commerce in a global economy. Ethical tensions and misunderstandings will arise in attempts to balance the conflicts that occur between acceptable behaviors and accepted cultures. Dealing with international parties who do not share American moral values or point of view will require careful guidance and understanding.

The challenges of the future are difficult and in many cases uncharted, but this is no reason to retreat from pursuing higher levels of ethical behavior. While it may be tempting to look for black-and-white solutions and the clear strictures of an earlier time, the complexities of our world today do not allow it. We are blessed to be living in a time and place in which diverse points of view, religions, cultures, and standards abound, occasioning lively debate about what it means to work and dwell in a moral community. For that purpose alone there is no doubt about why the business ethics imperative is here to stay. Here are six good reasons:

1. **At the very least, a solid ethical foundation is effective in establishing limits on conduct that is not proscribed by laws and regulations.** Laws cannot describe all events or doubts that will arise in the course of commerce. Company policies and codes of ethics can lay out additional guidelines.

2. **A program of ethics initiatives is definitely in the self-interest of every company and employee today.** White collar crime is conservatively estimated to cost businesses well in excess of $100 billion per year. Add to this figure the landscape of bankruptcies, lost jobs, restructuring, and declining stock values of companies that have become involved in ethical lapses, and, as the late Senator Everett Dirkson said, "Pretty soon you're talking about real money." Add to this also the specter of jail terms and increased financial penalties, thanks to the Federal Sentencing Guidelines, and you have real self-interest. Big crashes teach big lessons. Organizations are learning why ethics is important by watching what has happened to their peers.

3. **Institutions are discovering that an effective ethics program sets the tone for a superior corporate culture.** Business leaders looking to develop an environment in which there is a high level of trust and candor among individuals, in which disagreement and new ideas are encouraged and "groupthink" is discouraged, need look no further than to the open-

ness that results when employees receive solid training in ethical reasoning.

4.   **Ethics initiatives have a positive influence in the realm of relationships.** Ethics teaches us to think about how our conduct affects others, and is an effective business tool when so much of commerce involves preserving and strengthening relationships among customers, employees, suppliers, regulators and investors.

5.   **Ethics provides employees at all levels with the leadership skills they need as organizations require autonomous decision making from them.** Formerly, employees were taught what to do and how to do it. Occasionally they were taught what not to do. But command and control organizations are on their way out and employee empowerment and decentralization are in. Employees are being asked to make more decisions. Training in ethics provides employees with a deeper sense of moral awareness and gives them tools to make intelligent ethical business decisions. This training is needed today more than ever before when moral education at home, in school, or in religious institutions is lacking.

6.   **Finally, a solid moral foundation gives companies a competitive edge.** Business organizations are no longer idealized, left alone to produce goods and services. Times have changed. The rise of consumerism, environmentalism, civil rights, and the social responsibility movement, along with knowledgeable and aggressive financial media, have demonstrated that business institutions are as apt to be on the defensive as admired. And, should allegations of wrongdoing explode

across the front page, institutions that are admired today may be quickly vilified tomorrow. But it is equally true that if a company is known for its high ethical standards, it will continue to enjoy a measure of public admiration in times of crisis. This alone is a valid reason to develop and maintain **the ethical edge.**

About the Authors

Dawn-Marie Driscoll says she practiced "preventive legal medicine" while serving for many years as vice president of corporate affairs and general counsel of Filene's, the department store chain. At the time, her companywide program for ethical compliance consisted of brief anti-trust training, a business-card wallet reminder of basic Do's and Don'ts, and wide dissemination of her home phone number for employee assistance. The variety of ethical problems that arose over the years convinced her that a simple code of conduct was insufficient to change root causes such as misguided compensation structures and corporate culture deficiencies. Widely honored for her research and writing on career development and leadership, she is an independent director of several mutual funds and private companies, and a consultant. She is also an executive fellow and advisory board member of the Center for Business Ethics and serves on the board of governors of the Investment Company Institute.

Michael Hoffman was a young philosopher in 1974 and the newly appointed chairman of the Philosophy Department at Bentley College in Waltham, Mass. Since its founding in 1917, Bentley had built a reputation as an outstanding school for undergraduate students of business. Though a fine business school it was an odd home for an ethicist whose specialty was the esoteric theories of the 18th century German philosopher Immanuel Kant. Hoffman's solution was the creation of the Center for Business Ethics at Bentley. Twenty years later, Dr. Hoffman is an interna-

236

tionally recognized author and lecturer on business ethics, a sought-after expert witness in legal cases involving business ethics, and a founding member and past president of the Society for Business Ethics. He has played a leadership role in establishing the Ethics Officer Association, serving as its executive director for three years and now sits on its board of directors. He continues to serve as the executive director of the Center for Business Ethics and as a consultant to numerous organizations, assisting them in the building of a stronger ethical environment.

Edward S. Petry was the person the U.S. government turned to when it wanted to know which companies had the best developed ethics and compliance programs in the country. Dr. Petry identified 200 companies, all of which had issued written ethics standards and conducted extensive ethics training. Most also maintained internal helplines and had positioned corporate officers and high-level committees to oversee their companywide ethics and compliance initiatives. Many of the 200 companies are now members of the Ethics Officer Association that Dr. Petry leads as its executive director. As such, Dr. Petry works closely with managers who need practical advice to help them maintain their organization's **ethical edge.**

The Center for Business Ethics (founded in 1976) is the oldest and most internationally recognized institute for the study and exchange of ideas in business ethics among the worlds of academe, business, government, labor, and public interests. It is also the headquarters for and strategic partner of the **Ethics Officer Association,** an international professional association for ethics practitioners of for-profit as well as nonprofit organizations.

To order additional copies of *The Ethical Edge*, send a check for $24.95 for each book ordered plus $3 postage and handling for the first book, and $1 for each additional copy to:

MasterMedia Limited
17 East 89th Street
New York, NY 10128
(212) 546-7650
(800) 334-8232; please use MasterCard or VISA on phone orders
(212) 546-7638 (fax)

Dawn-Marie Driscoll, W. Michael Hoffman, and Edward Petry are available for speaking engagements. Please contact MasterMedia's Speaker's Bureau for availability and fee arrangements. Call Tony Colao at (800) 453-2887.

MasterMedia launches The Heritage Imprint— books that speak of courage, integrity and bouncing back from defeat. For the millions of Americans seeking greater purpose and meaning in their lives in difficult times, here are volumes of inspiration, solace and spiritual support.

The Heritage Imprint books will be supported by MasterMedia's full-service speakers' bureau, authors' media and lecture tours, syndicated radio interviews, national and co-op advertising and publicity.

Resiliency: How to Bounce Back Faster, Stronger, Smarter
Tessa Albert Warschaw, Ph.D. and Dee Barlow, Ph.D).

Resiliency is packed with practical techniques and insights on solving old problems in new ways. It also shows readers how to become more resilient in their personal and professional lives and teaches the skills for bouncing back from everyday stresses to surviving disastrous multiple losses. You will learn to enthusiastically embrace life. [$21.95, *Resiliency: How to Bounce Back Faster, Stronger, Smarter.* Hardbound ISBN 1-57101-021-1. A Book-of-the-Month, Free Spirit, and Quality Paperback Book Club selection.]

Journey Toward Forgiveness: Finding Your Way Home
BettyClare Moffatt, M.A., best-selling author of *Soulwork* and many other books.

Discover the difference forgiveness makes in your world. Learn to overcome anger, fear and resentment and live "in everincreasing joy and satisfaction and wonder." Step-by-step guidelines to forgiveness, meditation and prayer, action, healing and change. [$11.95, *Journey to Forgiveness: Finding Your Way Home.* Paperbound ISBN 1-57101-050-5.]

Heritage: The Making of an American Family
Dr. Robert B. Pamplin, Jr., with Gary K. Eisler, Jeff Sengstack and John Domini. Foreword by Dr. Norman Vincent Peale.

Fascinating saga of the Pamplin family, which has built one of the largest private fortunes in America. From the Crusades to today's multimillion-dollar corporation run by the author and his father, longtime head of the Georgia-Pacific Corporation. [$24.95, *Heritage: The Making of an American Family.* Hardbound ISBN 1-57101-021-1; $12.95 paperbound.]

Prelude to Surrender: The Pamplin Family and the Siege of Petersburg

Dr. Robert Pamplin, Jr., with Gary K. Eisler, Jeff Sengstack and John Domini.

"The special value of the family saga portrayed [here] lies not only in its engrossing tale of the remarkable Boisseau clan, but also in the insights shared when individual tales interesect with larger events."—Noah Andre Trudeau, Civil War historian. [$12.95 *Prelude to Surrender* Hardbound ISBN 1-57101-049-1.]

American Heroes: Their Lives, Their Values, Their Beliefs.

Dr. Robert B. Pamplin, Jr., with Gary K. Eisler.

Courage. Integrity. Compassion. The qualities of the hero still live in American men and women today—even in a world that can appear disillusioned. Share their stories of outstanding achievements. Discover the values that guide their lives and give courage to all of us. And learn some startling facts about what Americans really think of today's heroes, as revealed in a pioneering coast-to-coast survey.

Dr. Robert B. Pamplin, Jr., is a member of the Forbes 400, has been awarded numerous honorary degrees and has written 12 books. [$18.95, *American Heroes: Their Lives, Their Values, Their Beliefs.* Hardbound ISBN 1-57101-010-6.]

OTHER MASTERMEDIA BUSINESS BOOKS

To order additional copies of any MasterMedia book, send a check for the price of the book plus $2.00 postage and handling for the first book, $1.00 for each additional book to:

MasterMedia Limited
17 East 89th Street
New York, NY 10128
(212) 260-5600
(800) 334-8232 please use MasterCard or VISA on 1-800 orders
(212) 546-7638 (fax)

BEYOND SUCCESS: How Volunteer Service Can Help You Begin Making a Life Instead of Just a Living, by John F. Raynolds III and Eleanor Raynolds, C.B.E., is a unique how-to book targeted at business and professional people considering volunteer work, senior citizens who wish to fill leisure time meaningfully, and students trying out various career options. The book is filled with interviews with celebrities, CEOs, and average citizens who talk about the benefits of service work. ($19.95 cloth)

BOUNCING BACK: How to Turn Business Crises Into Success, by Harvey Reese. Based on interviews with entrepreneurs from coast to coast, this fascinating book contains cautionary tales that unfold with gripping suspense. Reese has discovered a formula for success that should be "must reading" for every new or budding entrepreneur. ($18.95 hardbound)

DARE TO CHANGE YOUR JOB—AND YOUR LIFE, by Carole Kanchier, Ph.D., provides a look at career growth and development throughout the life cycle. ($9.95 paper)

HOW TO GET WHAT YOU WANT FROM ALMOST ANYBODY, by T. Scott Gross, shows how to get great service, negotiate better prices, and always get what you pay for. ($9.95 paper)

LIFETIME EMPLOYABILITY: How to Become Indispensable, by Carole Hyatt, is both a guide through the mysteries of the business universe brought down to earth and a handbook to help you evaluate your attitudes, your skills, and your goals. Through expert advice and interviews of nearly 200 men and women whose lives have changed because their jobs or goals shifted, *Lifetime Employability* is designed to increase your staying power in today's down-sized economy. ($12.95 paper)

LEADING YOUR POSITIVELY OUTRAGEOUS SERVICE TEAM, by T. Scott Gross, provides a step-by-step formula for developing self-managing, excited service teams that put the customer first. T. Scott Gross tackles the question businesses everywhere are asking: "How do I get ordinary people to give world-class service?" A must-have for creating tomorrow's corporation today! ($12.95 paper)

THE LOYALTY FACTOR: Building Trust in Today's Workplace, by Carol Kinsey Goman, Ph.D., offers techniques for restoring commitment and loyalty in the workplace. ($9.95 paper)

MANAGING IT ALL: Time-Saving Ideas for Career, Family, Relationships, and Self, by Beverly Benz Treuille and Susan Schiffer Stautberg, is written for women who are juggling careers and families. Over two hundred career women (ranging from a TV anchorwoman to an investment banker) were interviewed. The book contains many humorous anecdotes on saving time and improving the quality of life for self and family. ($9.95 paper)

OUT THE ORGANIZATION: New Career Opportunities for the 1990's, by Robert and Madeleine Swain, is written for the millions of Americans whose jobs are no longer safe, whose companies are not loyal, and who face futures of uncertainty. It gives advice on finding a new job or starting your own business. ($12.95 paper)

POSITIVELY OUTRAGEOUS SERVICE: New and Easy Ways to Win Customers for Life, by T. Scott Gross, identifies what the consumers of the nineties really want and how businesses can develop effective marketing strategies to answer those needs. ($14.95 paper)

POSITIVELY OUTRAGEOUS SERVICE AND SHOWMANSHIP: Industrial Strength Fun Makes Sales Sizzle!!!!, by T. Scott Gross, reveals the secrets of adding personality to any product or service. ($12.95 paper)

REAL LIFE 101: The Graduate's Guide to Survival, by Susan Kleinman, supplies welcome advice to those facing "real life" for the first time, focusing on work, money, health, and how to deal with freedom and responsibility. ($9.95 paper)

A SEAT AT THE TABLE: An Insider's Guide for America's New Women Leaders, by Patricia Harrison, provides practical and insightful advice for women who are interested in serving on a board of directors, playing a key role in politics and becoming a policy- or opinion-maker in public or private sectors. This is one book every woman needs to own. ($19.95 hardbound)

SIDE-BY-SIDE STRATEGIES: How Two-Career Couples Can Thrive in the Nineties, by Jane Hershey Cuozzo and S. Diane Graham, describes how two-career couples can learn the difference between competing with a spouse and becoming a supportive power partner. Published in hardcover as *Power Partners.* ($10.95 paper, $19.95 cloth)

STEP FORWARD: Sexual Harassment in the Workplace, What You Need to Know, by Susan L. Webb, presents the facts for identifying the tell-tale signs of sexual harassment on the job, and how to deal with it. ($9.95 paper)

TAKING CONTROL OF YOUR LIFE: The Secrets of Successful Enterprising Women, by Gail Blanke and Kathleen Walas, is based on the authors' professional experience with Avon Products' Women of Enterprise Awards, given each year to outstanding women entrepreneurs. The authors offer a specific plan to help women gain control over their lives, and include business tips and quizzes as well as beauty and lifestyle information. ($17.95 cloth)

TEAMBUILT: Making Teamwork Work, by Mark Sanborn, teaches business how to improve productivity, without increasing resources or expenses, by building teamwork among employers. ($19.95 cloth)

A TEEN'S GUIDE TO BUSINESS: The Secrets to a Successful Enterprise, by Linda Menzies, Oren S. Jenkins, and Rickell R. Fisher, provides solid information about starting your own business or working for one. ($7.95 paper)

TWENTYSOMETHING: Managing and Motivating Today's New Work Force, by Lawrence J. Bradford, Ph.D., and Claire Raines, M.A., examines the work orientation of the younger generation, offering managers in businesses of all kinds a practical guide to better understand and supervise their young employees. ($22.95 cloth)

WORK WITH ME: How to Make the Most of Office Support Staff, by Betsy Zazary, shows you how to find, train, and nurture the "perfect" assistant and how to best utilize your support staff professionals. ($9.95 paper)